A STORY I AM IN

James Berry was born in 1924 and brought up in a tiny seaside village in Jamaica. He learnt to read before he was four years old, mostly from the Bible, which he often read aloud to his mother's friends. When he was 17, he went to work in America, but hated the way black people were treated there, and returned to Jamaica after four years. In 1948, he made his way to Britain, and took a job working for British Telecom.

One of the first black writers in Britain to achieve wider recognition, Berry rose to prominence in 1981 when he won the National Poetry Competition. His numerous books include two seminal anthologies of Caribbean poetry, *Bluefoot Traveller* (1976) and *News for Babylon* (Chatto, 1984). His latest book, *A Story I Am In: Selected Poems* (Bloodaxe Books, 2011), draws on six collections of poetry, including *Fractured Circles* (1979) and *Lucy's Letters and Loving* (1982) from New Beacon Books, *Chain of Days* (Oxford University Press, 1985), and *Hot Earth Cold Earth* (1995) and *Windrush Songs* (2007) from Bloodaxe. Windrush Songs was published to mark the 200th anniversary of the abolition of the slave trade.

He has published several books of poetry and short stories for children (from Hamish Hamilton, Macmillan, Puffin and Walker Books), and won many literary prizes, including the Smarties Prize (1987), the Signal Poetry Award (1989) and a Cholmondeley Award (1991). He was awarded the OBE in 1990. He lives in London.

JAMES BERRY
A STORY I AM IN
SELECTED POEMS

BLOODAXE BOOKS

Copyright © James Berry 1979, 1982, 1985, 1995, 2004, 2007, 2011

ISBN: 978 1 85224 917 5

First published 2011 by
Bloodaxe Books Ltd,
Highgreen,
Tarset,
Northumberland NE48 1RP.

www.bloodaxebooks.com
For further information about Bloodaxe titles
please visit our website or write to
the above address for a catalogue.

Cover design: Neil Astley & Pamela Robertson-Pearce.

Printed in Great Britain by
Bell & Bain Limited, Glasgow, Scotland.

For my friends

ACKNOWLEDGEMENTS

This edition includes poems selected from these previous collections by James Berry: *Fractured Circles* (1979) and *Lucy's Letters and Loving* (1982) published by New Beacon Books; *Chain of Days* (1985), published by Oxford University Press; and *Hot Earth Cold Earth* (1995) and *Windrush Songs* (2007), published by Bloodaxe Books. Most of poems included in the section *Poems for Children* are taken from his children's poetry collection *Only One of Me: Selected Poems* (Macmillan Children's Books, 2004).

In the section *Uncollected Poems*, 'A Redefining' was first published in *The Listener*, and 'Village Sex Lesson Number One' in *Ambit*. 'Rough Sketch Beginning' was originally published as a broadsheet in 1991 by Bernard Stone and Raymond Danowski, and published in another version as an illustrated book with the same title in 1996 by Harcourt Brace and Co.

Considerable thanks are due to Myra Barrs for her invaluable assistance in assembling this edition.

CONTENTS

13   Thinking About Poetry

from FRACTURED CIRCLES (1979)

17   I Spoke to Myself
17   Migrant in London
18   Travelling as We Are
19   Time Removed
20   Fractured Circles
21   Thoughts on My Father
23   White Child Meets Black Man
24   Boonoonoonoos
25   Deprivation
28   Outsider
29   Early Innocence
30   Moment of Love
30   You Two
31   Thoughts on My Mother

from LUCY'S LETTERS AND LOVING (1982)

35   Lucy's Letter
36   From Lucy: Englan Lady
37   From Lucy: Holiday Reflections
39   From Lucy: A Favour
40   From Lucy: New Generation
41   From Lucy: We Women
42   Loving
43   Flame and Water
43   Dialogue Between Two Large Village Women
44   Sweet Word Dem
45   A Sing-Sing fi Sileena
46   Ol Taata Nago
47   Meeting
48   Cut Way Feelins
48   Our Love Challenge
49   Taste of God
50   In Love

from CHAIN OF DAYS (1985)

53 Night Comes Too Soon
54 Caribbean Proverb Poems 1
55 Caribbean Proverb Poems 2
56 Chain of Days
60 Detention and Departure
61 Just Being
61 Going with All-Time Song
62 Fantasy of an African Boy
63 In God's Greatest Country, 1945
64 Notes on a Town on the Everglades, 1945
65 On an Afternoon Train from Purley to Victoria, 1955
66 In-a Brixtan Markit
67 Two Black Labourers on a London Building Site
68 Stories by Bodyparts
70 I am Racism
72 New World Colonial Child
76 Island Man
77 It's Me Man
78 Great Story
79 Confession
80 Benediction
80 Thinking Back on Yard Time
81 Memory
82 Nana Krishie the Midwife
83 Reclamation
86 Goodmornin Brodda Rasta
86 Approach and Response
87 Thinkin Loud-Loud
88 Calabash Tree
89 The Coming of Yams and Mangoes and Mountain Honey

from HOT EARTH, COLD EARTH (1995)

92 Spirits of Movement
93 Haiku Moments: 1
94 Hot Day Before My Time
94 Afternoon Sunhot
95 My Arrival
96 Haiku Moments: 2
97 My Cousin Rosetta
98 Early Days Thinking
99 Bluefoot Traveller

100 Faces Around My Father
104 Folk Proverbs Found Poems
105 In Our Year 1941 My Letter to you Mother Africa
109 Lion
110 What Is No Good?
111 Ol Style Freedom
112 I Am on Trial After Being Juror on a Black Man
116 Thoughts Going Home
118 A Schooled Fatherhood
119 Countryman O
120 Back Home Weddn Speech
120 Haiku Moments: 3
122 Meeting Mr Cargill on My Village Road
123 Starapple Time Starapple Trees
124 A Walk Through Kingston, Jamaica
125 Defendant in a Jamaican Court
126 Word of a Jamaican Laas Moment Them
126 Worse Than Poor
127 Villager's Independence: 1
128 Villager's Independence: 2
129 Woman at Waterhole
130 Masked People, One People
133 Everyday Traveller
133 Millennium Eyes
135 Words at My Mother's Funeral
137 People with Maps
137 Reply from Mother Africa
140 Reunion
142 Going About

from WINDRUSH SONGS (2007)

144 Wind-rush
144 Wash of Sunlight
145 Sitting up Past Midnight
146 Desertion
147 I African They Say
148 Old Slave Villages
148 Poverty Life
149 Poverty Ketch Yu and Hol Yu
150 Sea-Song One
150 Reasons for Leaving Jamaica
151 To Travel This Ship

152 A Dream of Leavin
152 Work Control Me Fadda Like a Mule
153 Reminiscence Voice
154 The Rock
155 Thinkin of Joysie
156 Fish Talk
156 Sun-Hot Drink
157 Empire Day
158 Old Slave Plantation Village Owner
159 Comparing Now with Ancestors' Travel from Africa
160 A Story I Am In
162 Mi Fight with Jack-Jack
163 How the Weak Manufactured Power for the Strong
164 Englan Voice
165 A Greater Oneness
166 New Space
167 In the Land and Sea Culture-crossed
168 Beginning in a City, 1948
170 Hymn to New Day Arriving

POEMS FOR CHILDREN

172 Seeing Granny
172 Listen Big Brodda Dead, Na!
173 Scribbled Notes Picked Up by Owners, and Rewritten
177 Black Kid in a New Place
177 A Story About Afiya
179 When I Dance
180 One
180 Boy Alone at Noon
181 Getting Nowhere
182 It Seems I Test People
183 What Do We Do with a Variation
184 Me Go a Granny Yard
185 Jamaican Song
186 Hurricane
187 Isn't My Name Magical?
188 Childhood Tracks
189 Rain Friend
190 Okay, Brown Girl, Okay
191 Innercity Youth Walks and Talks
193 Trick a Duppy
193 Love Is Like Vessel

194 People Equal
195 Gobble-Gobble Rap
196 A Nest Full of Stars
197 Caribbean Playground Song
198 Flop, Clonk, Bump, Zoom
198 Tall, Wide and Heavy

UNCOLLECTED POEMS

200 A Redefining
200 Childhood Memory
201 A Father's Vigil
202 Fatherhood
203 Cos somtin mek it so
204 Ol Nasty Mout
202 Village Sex Lesson Number One
206 Whatever happened to Miranda?
206 God to Me
207 Absorbing
208 Rough Sketch Beginning

Thinking About Poetry

This book contains a selection from all five of my books of poetry for adults – and a small selection of poems from my four books of poetry for children. Poetry has been important to me all my life. I like the thinking that comes out of it, it often shakes my knowing into a wider vision. Although I have written in other forms it's always this form that I've come back to.

Poetry began to matter to me when I was very young. I was exposed to two main languages from babyhood – the standard English of the Bible and the prayerbook that I heard every Sunday at church, with all its rhythms and sounding patterns; and the tunes of everyday Jamaican language, with its sayings and proverbs, its special dialect words with their African connections, its expression of a roots culture. These experiences gave me a strong awareness of language.

Poetry is a form that urges you to dig deeply into varied life. It urges you to disentangle things and understand them. It explores attitudes, nature, the world and all its connections. It is a form of cultural assessment, a means of assessing groups of people and their ways. It offers you other depths and levels of thinking about everyday being. I feel that it opens your mind.

Going about writing a poem is like learning a particular way of putting on your shirt comfortably. It's like learning any kind of trade, you have to feel comfortably at home with your tools, words. In making a poem the mind wants to understand more about depth of being, about life. The language is chosen to stir the reader to be thoughtful – poetry invites you to walk or sit and think, to be focused on life. When a poem works well it has different levels of reflection, it is a deep meditation.

For me the most important thing about writing a poem is trying to explore the subject fully. It's like penetrating and trying to understand the workings of the sun, or water, or the movements of animals and birds. I look for subject-matter that stirs me, my first casting of an eye on a poem is always to find out what the subject is about – what questions does it throw up? Ted Hughes is a poet whose language takes you into depth of thinking about a subject – you are stirred to stop and think.

A good poem is one that works and tells you something about life and opens itself to an understanding of variation and being. When these things engage you, something begins to grow. Kamau Brathwaite's poetry matters to me because he explores different aspects of Caribbean being, our history and mentality. Often in rhythms of the drum, blues, jazz or gospel, Brathwaite's poetry helped to create a new awareness of a people's culture that was once considered empty.

It's not only the formation of words but the thought in a poem that matters to me. It's the ideas in a poem that can make a difference, that can suprise you in a wonderful way. Walcott's poetry does that for me, he expresses human experience in a way that shakes you, excites you. He's deeply involved with interpreting African, European and Caribbean experience. He has a great intellectual grasp. And he was also born in love with language – it's his obsession – to see, smell, hear, taste and express all this through words. He makes language work for him, he bends it, he knows its crevices and echoes. He clarifies the Caribbean landscape of island and sea, with its history and people. Through his obsession he has made the Caribbean the centre of a whole literary world. His passion knows the human need to expand itself, to be more, not to be confined by geography or race.

Poetry is a form of music that stirs connections. It's the human experience in discovery. It opens up ideas that you didn't know existed until you tried to put them into words. Writing poetry is a way of striving to see as deeply as possible, as widely as possible, as accurately as possible. Because language does all this for us.

JAMES BERRY

Fractured Circles

(1979)

I Spoke to Myself

You can't settle on the ground
like an earth loving rock.
You can't stay still
like a chopped down log.

I woke up and found
I marked earth
with my lying down.
I saw I hid and rotted.

I saw business of time
worked on me,
like disposable waste.

I arrested time:
I moved,
unaware of kept movements
to devour me

Migrant in London

Sand under we feet long time.
Sea divided for we, you know,
how we turned stragglers to the Mecca.

An' in mi hangin' drape style
I cross worl' centre street, man.
An' busy traffic hoot horns.

I see Big Ben strike
the mark of my king town.
Pigeons come perch on mi shoulder,
roun' great Nelson feet

I stan' in the roar, man,
in a dream of wheels
a-vibrate shadows.
I feel how wheels hurry in wheels.

I whisper, man you mek it.
You arrive.
Then sudden like, quite loud I say,
'Then whey you goin' sleep tenight?'

Travelling As We Are

They hadn't launched their briefing.
They were still cocooned in
the flame of their tongues –
Martin Luther King, Malcolm X,
James Baldwin, etcetera.

My rage unignited
I sat enclosed underground,
British among Britons, only
there, in the nearly empty London
train, going to work.

   Look, Mummy, look, a nigger. Mummy
   niggers can sit here. Mummy, look.

She didn't glance once.
She wouldn't expose a wink.
She withdrew, hooded skilfully
till her southern American voice
trailed a sigh:

   So they can, Tim.
   So they can.

I knew the flight of mind. My
demeaning stressed her excellence,
as I had known it
in her southern US town.

But this is Europe, Mummy. How come
niggers live here too?

Tim and Sally Jane, when you get home
ask your daddy. You ask your daddy.

Here loaded together we
mattered much to each other,
our tomorrow and yesterday now,
stirring each other, without
a word or glance reciprocated.

An aching hatred left the train
with me. All day suspicion
spurred me. I spoke hastily.
Retaliation wrestled me.

Time Removed

I go on and on in England
and walk no ground untrodden.

Landscapes are checkered –
tamed out of new years
and recurring generations.

Compulsive hands have shaped
bordered fields
out of scrub,
rivers' faces with bridge,
edifices for trees towering
lands now railed and tarred.

Animals are not bony and bare.
Wheels quicken time –
through a late summer
staying fresh as spring.

And here
just as jungles hold my love
every whiff of air evokes a time
like the horse my father left
and I after ten years away
found the greyhaired skeleton
neighing to me,
like these days do,
in memories too overlaid to touch.

Fractured Circles

my life once
a dancing leaf
took a blade through her stance

my life once
a seeking whale
spun it out in a bloody sea

my life once
a looking eagle
drifted in wing ensnared

my life once
a searching lion
flew when a shot turned her paws

my life once
a busy fox
rushed from the fangs of hounds

my life once
a hiding worm
leapt from flesh of fruit and jaws

my life once
a hippopotamus
gave the gun stop a pale red lake

my life once
a lamb
dealt a heart to cooking pots

my life once
a green man
wandered from white sheets

life I rage
in fractured circles
fill me a life

Thoughts on My Father

You are boned clean now.
You are lost like dice and teeth.
Don't bother knock
I won't represent you.

A sound brain you were,
your body a mastery,
but no turning into any stepping stone
or handing anybody a key.

Simply it hurts that needing
we offended you
and I judge you by lack.

Playing some well-shaped shadow
the sun alone moved,
you wouldn't be mixed with cash
or the world's cunning.

So perfectly exclusive,
you tantalised me.
You split our home in passions.
Every year we were more blunted.

I knew nowhere.
My eyes looked out from you
my first god.

Omnipotence breathed
come boy come
to hungrybelly revelations.

Lift your hat to doom
boy in the manner that roadside
weeds are indestructible.

Stubborn tides you echo.

I moved your sterile tones
from my voice.
I lifted your mole
from my back.

You scar me man,
but I must go over you again and again.
I must plunge my raging eyes
in all your steady enduring.

I must assemble material
of my own
for a new history.

White Child Meets Black Man

She caught me outside a London
suburban shop, I like a giraffe
and she a mouse. I tried to go
but felt she stood
lovely as light on my back.

I turned with hello
and waited. Her eyes got
wider but not her lips.
Hello I smiled again and watched.

She stepped around me
slowly, in a kind of dance,
her wide eyes searching
inch by inch up and down:
no fir no scales no feathers
no shell. Just a live silhouette,
wild and strange
and compulsive
till mother came horrified.

'Mummy is his tummy black?'
Mother grasped her and swung
toward the crowd. She tangled
mother's legs looking back at me.
As I watched them birds were singing.

Boonoonoonoos

You so full of you
  fe me
  I lose miself
  fe you
Boonoonoonoos gal
  you so roun an sweet

You consida you so hard
  fe me
  I get betta than me
  fe you
Boonoonoonoos gal
  you so roun an sweet

Everyday like palmlimbs a-touch
  in rain an sun-hot breeze
  we go greener an greener
  fe we
Boonoonoonoos gal
  you so roun an sweet

Deprivation

Again this extreme of time.
Rivers are dry.
River rocks look sea deserted.
Under white pestles of sky
earth is refuge free.

   Why
   this furnace of air
   this quiet elemental fever?

On and on scarcity defaces,
in odours of earth's reversal.
Crows wait on forked branch.

No support for green,
none for blood.
Crust moves away from crust.
Lands gape like faces.
Ground gapes gagged
with leaves curled crisply.

Nose to nose the shrivelled
cattle cry to a vanished pool.
And flame from mouth
of sky is steady.

   Why
   this furnace of air
   this quiet elemental fever?

Here between lost bones,
lost feathers lost horns,
the skeleton dog chews a beetle.

And since no leaves
to give voices,
no wind is around.

Since all commands call death,
no answer is about.

The sun stages
its art objects
before its eye:
its painted nudes are numb,
breathing quiet resignation.

People are tired
sheltered by sticks
leaved with vultures.
People are positioned
with tiredness.

    Why
    this furnace of air
    this quiet elemental fever?

No one remembers
the last rain
or the last green fruit.

All are odd exhibits:
children indented like raisins:
all faces black masks
edged and sunken.

Faces carry one
communal knowing:
there is no water
in the sky
or at hand
or beyond reach underground.
There is no water.

There is a sacred acquiescence,
a vigilance
that no one can break
from the many postures
that blend a landscape.

It is the abstinence,
the unobstructed abstinence
time prepared,
with no drumming
no horn playing
no backslapping
no handgrasping.

It is the dull time
in the dazzling time,
the deathly sacrificial time
for water unreachable,
for water wasted
for water not stored
for water not given
for water not recycled
for water unreceived.

It is where the sun
beats up the halfdead,
the girls not beautified
and the boys not caring,
except for false rumbles.

    Why
    this furnace of air
    this quiet elemental fever?

Far clouds could clear
and there's never a waiting
without a moving
without a moving to some end.

    Why
    this furnace of air
    this quiet elemental fever?

Outsider

If you see me lost on busy streets,
my dazzle is sun-stain of skin,
I'm not naked with dark glasses on
saying barren ground has no oasis:
it's that cracked up by extremes
I must hold self
together with extreme pride.

If you see me lost in neglected
woods, I'm no thief eyeing trees
to plunder their stability
or a moaner shouting at air:
it's that voices in me rule
firmer than my skills, and sometimes
among men my stubborn hurts
leave me like wild dogs.

If you see me lost on forbidding
wastelands, watching dry flowers
nod, or scraping a tunnel
in mountain rocks, I don't open
a trail back into time:
it's that a monotony
like the Sahara seals my enchantment.

If you see me lost on long
footpaths, I don't set traps
or map out arable acres:
it's that I must exhaust twigs
like limbs with water divining.

If you see me lost in my sparse
room, I don't ruminate
on prisoners and falsify
their jokes, and go on about
prisons having been perfected
like a common smokescreen of mind:
it's that I moved
my circle from ruins
and I search to remake it whole.

Early Innocence

Remorse never came near it
when we sank puppies and kittens
or when we whacked worms
to see how pieces wriggled.

It could have been called pure
how we tested birds-egg thinness
with knocks, and how we took
halffull bags of fledglings
from summer woods.

Doubt came nowhere near
laughter ringing round us,
when we showed the sun
the weakling's willy, and made
the spastic boy eat dirt.

Nothing like trouble was about
when we caught and raced
the neighbour's pony, over
and over sultry pastureland
and swore with tears
the beast bathed in the pond.

But then early fun had not become
an expert's guide to living
to make the mute and the weak pay,
in jungle or city.

Every fish we hooked we cooked.
Every bird we shot was seasoned.

Moment of Love

Sweetrose Sweetrose you pretty
Lawd Lawd hol' this time
hol' it like Joshua still the sun
She lyin' here I full
I brimful with joy
   brimful with joy –
no empty pocket on me to drag me
no lockedhead of mine to fail me
no government debate to bug me
Only she lyin' here needin' not a word
An' I sing sweeter than any blackbird
Sweetrose Sweetrose you pretty
Stay good an' don' get baby
   Stay good an' don' get baby

You Two

What a couple you are
   always at peace and war
You put each other down
   you build each other up

You lie like hell to each other
   you pour honest hearts to each other
You love each other in tears
   you explode and smash up the wares

You laugh like claps of thunder
   you sit together full of wonder
You have conned each other
   you have redeemed each other

You both escaped
   you both reappeared
You talk deeply in bed
   you scorn each other as dead

You damaged each other
   you nursed each other
You undervalue each other
   you overrate each other

You fought off the world for each other
What a couple you are

Thoughts on My Mother

Bare trees turn the mind
to palm leaves a-rattle round
an open house with shadows wild
about a boy stretching sinews
in the stings and wash
of your voice your hands your eyes

Your oiled hand makes a cross
on my belly, and all
pain goes

Caretaker of my beginnings your echoes
pull me in and out from where many
bare feet slap earth floor,
secure, under the thatch cured in smoke
old as granpuppa, your domain
wattled in, with smells mixed with
ginger, nutmeg and pimento berries
and old sweat of donkey padding

And your pestle a-crush woodfired
coffeebeans and cocoabeans
with cinnamon, and corn and cassava,
and no food is ever the same
after your salted pepper spice-up
from a sapling table

December is stuck in gardens
and bed blankets here
but red hibiscus opens up
the playmates' wood-and-straw
place, and the song in your hair
like your patience I could
never have, with your luxury
iced water in a calabash

Woman
you hang no accomplishments:
it's one late gold ring a-flash
your only jewel, yet eight people's
habits and clothes-fabric were
like a map in your palm

Frost winds in England try
to skin me white: you are
warm, your face
wet in sweat, black in sunlight
as you dig, chop or stitch,
with feet bare like
the scorpions and centipedes,
that I may let go my tasselled roots
the sun pulls upward.

Lucy's Letters and Loving

(1982)

Lucy's Letter

Things harness me here. I long
for we labrish bad. Doors
not fixed open here.
No Leela either. No Cousin
Lil, Miss Lottie or Bro'-Uncle.
Dayclean doesn' have cockcrowin'.
Midmornin' doesn' bring
Cousin-Maa with her naseberry tray.
Afternoon doesn' give a ragged
Manwell, strung with fish
like bright leaves. Seven days
play same note in London, chile.
But Leela, money-rustle regular.

Me dear, I don' laugh now,
not'n' like we thunder claps
in darkness on verandah.
I turned a battery hen
in 'lectric light, day an' night.
No mood can touch one
mango season back at Yard.
At least though I did start
evening school once.
An' doctors free, chile.

London isn' like we
village dirt road, you know
Leela: it a parish
of a pasture-lan' what
grown crisscross streets,
an' they lie down to my door.
But I lock myself in.
I carry keys everywhere.
Life here's no open summer,
girl. But Sat'day mornin' don'
find me han' dry, don' find me face
a heavy cloud over the man.

An' though he still have
a weekend mind for bat'n'ball
he wash a dirty dish now, me dear.
It sweet him I on the Pill.
We get money for holidays
but there's no sun-hot
to enjoy cool breeze.

Leela, I really a sponge
you know, for traffic noise,
for work noise, for halfway
intentions, for halfway smiles,
for clockwatchin' an' col' weather.
I hope you don' think I gone
too fat when we meet.
I booked up to come an' soak
the children in daylight.

labrish: to gossip without restraint

From Lucy: Englan' Lady

You ask me 'bout the lady. Me dear,
old centre here still shine
with Queen. She affec' the place
like the sun: not comin' out oft'n
an' when it happ'n everybody's out
smilin', as she wave a han'
like a seagull flyin' slow slow.

An' you know she come from
dust free rooms an' velvet
an' diamond. She make you feel
this on-an'-on town, London,
where long long time deeper than mind.
An' han's after han's die away,
makin' streets, putt'n' up bricks,
a piece of brass, a piece of wood
an' plantin' trees: an' it give
a car a halfday job gett'n' through.

An' Leela, darlin', no, I never
meet the Queen in flesh. Yet
sometimes, deep deep, I sorry for her.

Everybody expec' a show
from her, like she a space touris'
on earth. An' darlin', unless
you can go home an' scratch up
you' husban', it mus' be hard
strain keepin' good graces for
all hypocrite faces.

Anyhow, me dear, you know what
ole time people say,
'Bird sing sweet for its nest'.

From Lucy: Holiday Reflections

I'm here an' not here. Me head's
too full of mornin' sun
an' sea soun' an' voices
echoin' words this long long
time I never have.

Seeing home again, Leela chile,
I bring back a mind to Englan'
tha's not enough to share. For how
I eat a mango under tree,
a soursop ripened for me,
a pawpaw kept, brings back
the whole taste of sunshine
an' how our own love ripen.

O I glad to see hard times
ease off some faces a little.
I glad to see the stream still
goin' in the gully, though
where it gives up to sea
is a different face now.

Big fig tree gone as ghost.
Whole breed of nana midwives
gone. Givin'-for-not'n' gone
mixed with cash. I had to ask
a–where walled bank of fire an'
wood ashes gone from kitchen
for paraffin smell? Then I see
me head lost the account
of everything and everybody.

I meet a young face I get
the pain we don't know each other.
An' I see Cousin John fine-shin boy
stretch up to sixfoot man. I see
Puppa is bones in the groun',
Mumma can't see to climb mount'n
lan'. An' smellin' of pee, Aunty
Meg's in bed all through sunhot.
Then old Granny Lyn an' kids have
no regular man voice about.

Leela, sweetheart, I glad glad
I came home. I glad you still
have wasp waist an', funny,
that you' hair still short.
You see how food fill me out:
I promise to slim.

I glad you don't grow bitter.
I glad how the sun still ripen
evenin', so strong in colour.
An' there, where I did go
to school with one piece of book,
I came, I walked in darkness,
an' it was a soothin' blot.

Too many sea waves passed between
us, chile. Let us remind the other,
'Length of time gets length of rope buried'.

From Lucy: A Favour

Leela, darlin', as we did talk,
go an' see the piece of lan'
Cousin Man-Man buy for me. I glad
it near the sea an' not mount'n
lan'. It planted well I hear.
Coconuts, bananas, sugar cane
an' some food growin'. A good
house spot is there, what I will
get raised up little by little.

I more peaceful I get that lan'.
Money here is too dry: can't
turn it in a pig or goat, only
comforts, what make me ashame
sometimes. Ashame too how
neighbours supply dustbins
with loaves, with half chickens,
with good clothes.

Nowadays I don't eat in a day
or two, I sing to meself. I think
of air we breathe, water
we drink an' sun that shine.
I don't let the man touch
me V-centre place.

Darlin', a parcel on the way
for you. Go an' see the piece
of lan' for me. Soon I'll come
again an' walk on it
in breeze what touch the sun
an' swing coconut limbs.

Walk good, Leela, chile.
'Walk-good keeps good spirit.'

From Lucy: New Generation

Yes, Leela, full teenagers now,
Tony an' Sharon. An' free at school
to work or squander time.
Thank God they hol' their own.
They body blemish free
an' you'd think they have no fear.

I did want them know the Bible,
know Shakespeare. Me dear, they
pity me. They say I still missing
links, I still don' understan'
world without black gods isn'
in worlds without end. The Buddha,
Mohammed, Jah, all
know the way they say.

They different breed, me dear.
The heads are Afro style.
They wear patches on the bum
to show they side with the poor.

Westindies is jus' a place parents
born: Bob Marley's their only thought
in it. 'Beat' sounds hypnotise them.
Beat-makers give them religion.

An' it's their joke I teachin'
me English neighbour Westindian Talk.
They eat'n' curry-an'-rice now
I say, they need little
Westindies Talk to season it.
They laugh at me an' say I funny.

Me dear, we all
lookin', lookin', lookin'.
Remember, 'One han' washes the other'.

From Lucy: We Women

Leela, chile, you ask how
we women in Brit'n makin'
out. Well, darlin', you know
how at home the man never
did see we as flower
or toy or blessed virgin.
You know how he did see we
more so a donkey an' breedin'
body an' pupp'a an' granny.
Well, me dear, over here,
it prove now that she who have
a big han' in money an' food
an' sex is in business, girl.
Is the handout from husban'
did keep women back. With own
cash, she right there
handlin' own firs' item.

Listen one male chauvinist-pig
writer, in newspaper other
day: 'It psychological
how women wear more trousers
now, an' show real size
of they bum; it make them
feel secure, as equal competitor
pushin' theyself more at the top.'

Darlin', listen, though I don'
join yet, I go sometime to hear
some revolutionary white
sistas, who shut the door on
the opposite sex. It really
is relief to let rip
on men, me dear, even me
who didn' know she need it.

The sistas ask we all to rejec'
toy an' flower an' virgin
image, me dear. No more
worship as goddess they say.

No more tricks by men
to create an' control an' enjoy
a devil-worl' to theyself.

All the same, Leela, it still
break my heart to see
a whole-loaf in rubbish bin.
I still not sure it right
how I do no clothes patchin' now.
An', darlin', I mus' tell you,
but don' laugh, I still feel rude
when I shave me armpit.

Darlin', remember,
'When fire an' water keep
good company, everybody can live'.

Loving

If loving is a river
embraced in the ground
and is the face of barefeet
kissing the ground as it goes
it is longing in movement

If loving is a rock
sitting in the earth
and is the deep root
of a tree stilled blissfully
it is steadiness

If loving is a pig
wallowing in soft wet earth
and is a woman's body
supine in sunlight wash
it is discovery

Flame and Water

She steams him up
she makes him hot
she makes him rage
he boils over
he floods her
he extinguishes her

She regathers
she heats him
she makes him vapour
he regathers
he sprays her
he makes her smoulder

She regathers
she stings him steadily
she leaves him to cool
he regathers
he keeps up
steady drops on her flame

She warms him he wets her
She warms him he wets her
they carry on
and carry on
wishing for the secret
of balance

Dialogue Between Two Large Village Women

Vergie mi gal, yu know
wha overtek mi?

   Wha, Bet-Bet darlin?

Yu know de downgrow bwoy
dey call Runt?

Everybody know de lickle
forceripe wretch.

Well mi dear, de bwoy put
question to mi.

   Wha? Wha yu sey?

Yeahs – put question to mi
big-big woman, who could be
him mummah over and over.

   Laad above. Didn yu bounce
   de damn lickle ramgoat face?

Mi hol him an mi shake
de lickle beas like
to kill de wretch.
An yu know wha happn?

   No.

De lickle brute try fi kiss mi.

Sweet Word Dem

Yu tink mi a somtn fi eat
ow yu a-look pon mi so?

      Nobody did evva eat
      flame-tree bloom
      or try to swallah
      dazzle of de sun.

Yu full a sweet word dem.
Supposn mi is trouble?

      Modesty is always
      de sign
      of a generous heart.

If even I tell yu probly
mi sweetnis av a sting?

    If bees didn av sting
    dey wouldn a-keep
    any honey fi deyself.

Talk to mi again noh.
I like ow yu look.
I like ow yu show-off
wid wha I cahn see.

    I goin walk wid yu now.

An I not goin call de police.

A Sing-Sing fi Sileena

Sileena head dry
Sileena head dry
but yu noh ask why
an yu noh ask why
cos Sileena full yu eye
    o yu noh ask why
    an yu noh ask why
    cos Sileena full yu eye

Sileena talk shy
Sileena talk shy
but yu noh ask why
an yu noh ask why
cos Sileena big mout sweet
    o yu noh ask why
    an yu noh ask why
    cos Sileena big mout sweet

dry head: extremely short-haired; usually 'dry head woman'.

Sileena leg fine
Sileena leg fine
but yu noh ask why
an yu noh ask why
cos Sileena bubby big
   o yu noh ask why
   an yu noh ask why
   cos Sileena bubby big

Sileena born broke
Sileena born broke
but yu noh ask why
an yu noh ask why
cos Sileena botty high
   o yu noh ask why
   an yu noh ask why
   cos Sileena botty high

Sileena busy
Sileena busy
but yu noh ask why
an yu noh ask why
cos Sileena full up house wid lickle somody
   o yu noh ask why
   an yu noh ask why
   cos Sileena full up house wid lickle somody dem o

Ol Taata Nago

To sweat out somebody bad fever
ol Taata Nago boil bush an bark
like ol woman a poun spice up cocobeans.

An him not frightn a any sorefoot lookin
like a bad cave in a bad stink.

Him not frightn to wrestle devil
out a bawlin mad man grindin teeth.

Him not frightn to pull out
bad teeth with him pliers.

Him not frightn to get news from we good dead
or sen away bad duppy who throw stone
in a dark night pon housetop.

Taata Nago not known to turn back any blow
of obeah, ask to be turn back.

We only joke Taata Nago how
pushin seventy he boil him own
strong-back drink

an still have
baby born every year.

But we know Taata love
havin a houseful
cos Taata love the gettin of children.

duppy: ghost who harms the living; *obeah:* witchcraft.

Meeting

Your wild body is empty and still I said
    I have hunted you she said – why?
I desired you I said
    But you were repugnant to me she said
That was the tribal eye I said
    I want to dance as Africans do she said
I want to roar like Shakespeare I said
    I have hunted you – why?
I spoke in you silently
    But I was frightened of you
That was taught emotion
    I wish my skin was ebony like yours she said
I wish mine appleblossom like yours I said
    Shall we meet again?
O much closer than earth and sky

Cut-Way Feelins

Yu know him gone.
Children we know him gone.
Him gone lef de sun
fi walk tru yard
widdout him back-a it.

Yu know him gone.
We know him gone.
Him gone lef stars like spears
from roof holes in we eyes.

Naked big shoulda not here –
dohn come an eat we food,
dohn come an mek mi curse
a–beg a lovin look.

Yu know him gone.
Children we know him gone.
Clay bowl dohn av
shavin suds pon Sunday now.
Logs dem alone hol up a house.

Our Love Challenge
(for Mary)

Maybe designs for conflict worked me
when I exploded on the stage
with a kept slave anger
thoughtless you'd walk out wounded

So full in time I let out
my raging hungry dogs
who threatened me

You take it I accuse you
of seizing children's keep
with whip with cruel lordship
you say I invest in vengeance
I storm you with ancestors' sins

You cut all lines to me
you go to old fires behind barriers
I like an outlaw withdraw

But we linger together again
suppositions recede
we slowly become this new area
between killing sun and killing ice
in battles against incoming tides

Taste of God

Mi drink mi goady-water in a sun-hot work sweat
mi suck a soff ripe mango or naseberry
mi eat a piece a turn-breadfruit pon Sunday
mi suck a piece a juicy beef bone
mi get in a mi rum an talkin good
mi stan up a-sing a hymn in a church deep deep
mi have mi hardnis in a mi woman soffnis –
everytime man like so I taste de God-Amighty

In Love

I love the love turned movement
love the love turned enjoyment

I love the love turned light and seeing
love the love turned night and knowing

I love the love turned mother
love the love turned father

I love the love turned summer
love the love turned water

I love the love turned fire
love the love turned desire

I love the love turned diaphanous air in a whirl
love the love turned girl

I love the love turned joy
love the love turned boy

I love the love turned taste of sun
love the love turned smell of rain

I love the love turned death and birth
love the love turned earth

I love the love turned solace when alone
love the love turned stone

I love the love of love
and how I am a song of love

FROM

Chain of Days

(1985)

Night Comes Too Soon

Here now skyline assembles fire.
The sun collects up to leave.
Its bright following paled,
suddenly all goes. Dusk rushes
in, like door closed on windowless room
Children go a little sad.

Fowls come in ones and groups
and fly up with a cry
and settle, in warm air branches.
Tethered pigs are lounging
in dugout ground.

Muzzled goat kids make muffled
cries. Cows call calves locked away.
Last donkey-riders come homeward
calling 'Good night!'
Children go a little sad.

Knives-making from flattened
big nails must stop. Kite ribs
of tied sticks must not develop.
Half shapes growing into bats
and balls, into wheels and tops
must cease by night's veto.

And, alone on shelves, in clusters
on the ground in corners, on
underhouse ledges, these
lovable embryos
don't grow in sleeptime.
Children go a little sad.

Bats come out in swarms.
Oil lamps come up glowing
all through a palmtree village.
Everybody'll be indoors
like logs locked up.
Children go a little sad.

Caribbean Proverb Poems 1

Dog mornin prayer is, Laard
wha teday, a bone or a blow?

Tiger wahn fi nyam pickney, tiger sey
he could-a swear e woz puss.

If yu cahn mek plenty yeyewater
fi funeral, start a-bawl early mornin.

Caribbean Proverb Poems 2

1

Hungrybelly an Fullbelly
dohn walk same pass.

Fullbelly always a-tell Emptybelly
'Keep heart'.

2

Yu fraid fi yeye
yu cahn nyam cowhead.

Yeye meet yeye
an man fraid!

3

Yu si yu neighbour beard
ketch fire, yu tek water
an wet fi yu.

When lonely man dead,
grass come grow a him door.

4

Satan may be ol
but Satan not bedriddn.

Man who is all honey,
fly dem goin nyam him up.

nyam: eat; *pickney:* child or children; *ysye:* eye.

Chain of Days

In the spicing the salting and the blackening
I'm poling up in fires of summerlight.
A tree blooms from my umbilical cord.
I look for a touch from every eye.
Darkness the wide shawl with sun's heat,
my mother's songs go from wooden walls.
Humming birds hovering
hibiscus nodding
I dance in the eyes of an open house.

    On a summer road under swinging palms
    a chain of days showed me bewildered.

Taking the drumming of the sea on land
I take the rooted gestures,
I take the caged growing.
Little lamps merely tarnish
a whole night's darkness.
Our stories bring out Rolling-Calves
with eyes of fire and trail of long chain.
I look for a sign in every face,
particularly in my father's face.

A joy is trapped in me.
Voices of rainbow birds shower my head.
I decapitate my naked toe.
My eye traps warm dust.
I'm born to trot about delivering
people's words and exchanged favours
or just grains of corn or sugar or salt.

Scooped water dances
in the bucket perched on me.
My bellows of breath make leaps of flames.
I muzzle goat kids in raging sunsets
and take their mother's milk in morning light.

Beaten there to remember I know nothing
I run to school with a page of book
and clean toenails and teeth.

All my homestead eggs go to market.
Farthings are the wheels that work my world.
My needs immaterial, I know I'm alien.

My father stutters before authority.
His speeches have no important listener.
No idea that operates my father
invites me to approach him.
And I wash my father's feet in sunset
in a wooden bowl.

And my father's toothless mother is wise.
My father coaxes half dead cows
and horses and roots in the ground;
he whispers to them sweetly and shows
the fine animal coat he persuaded to shine;
he pulls prized yams from soft earth
like big babies at birth
to be carried to rich tables.

Confused and lonely I sulk.
Companioned and lost I laugh.
I fill hunger with games.

On a summer road under swinging palms
a chain of days showed me bewildered.

I go to the wood
it is a neighbour.
I go to the sea
it is a playground.
I circle track marked hills.
I circle feet cut flatlands.

I turn rocks I turn leaves.
I hunt stone and nut marbles in woods.
I rob pigeon pairs from high trees.
Wasps inflate my face for a soursop.
I beat big nails into knives.
Tops and wheels and balls come from wood.
Yet movement and shape mystify:
I am tantalised.

I understand I'm mistaken
to know I'm truly lovable, and that
my lovable people are truly lovable.
I understand something makes me alien.
I wonder why so many seedlings wither
like my father's words before authority.

Wondering, dreaming, overawed, I sit
in the little room with faces like mine.
Low lamp light spreads a study
of the past on our faces.
I sleep with the purple of berries
on my tongue, and I warm thin walls.

On a summer road under swinging palms
a chain of days showed me bewildered.

I keep back the pig's squeal
or the young ram's holler
when my father takes out their balls
with his own razor.
Water I pour washes my father's hands.
I wish my father would speak.
I wish my father would use
magic words I know he knows.
I wish my father would touch me.

Past winds have dumped
movements my ancestors made.
I dread my father's days
will boomerang on me.
I want to stop time and go with time.
In the hills alone I call to time.
My voice comes back in the trees
and wind. Why isn't there the idea
to offer me as sacrifice like Abraham's son?

My sister goes and washes
her breasts in the river.
Like a holy act I wash
in my brothers' dirty water.

On a summer road under swinging palms
a chain of days showed me bewildered.

My mother's dead granny brings
medicines to her in dreams.
My mother is a magician.
My mother knows how to ignore my father.
My mother puts food and clothes
together out of air. Bush and bark and grasses
work for my mother. She stops
the wickedest vomiting. She tells you
when you haven't got a headache at all.
In the pull of my mother's voice
and hands she stings and she washes me.

Put me in bright eye of sunlight
in shadows under broad hats,
on hillside pulling beans,
or chopping or planting,
I am restful with my mother.

The smell of sunny fields in my clothes
I meet my mother's newborn in the secret
birth room strong with asafetida.
I say goodbye touching my mother's mother
in the yard, her cold face
rigid toward the sky.

Quickfooted in the summer
I come over dust and rocks.
Echo after echo leaves me
from the edge of the sea,
from the edge of the sea.

Rolling-Calves: monstrous evil spirits, in the form
of calves, who haunt the countryside at night.

Detention and Departure

I shouldn't live, you know, man.
I shouldn't live,
too much hunger devoured me,
too many lacks hit me in
and stamped me down
all heels over head long long time.

I washed up here washed-up,
an overdone case, man,
rolled from ship of fire,
tongue clipped,
steps short.

A dry stick sun-charged man,
I powered axe,
powered crowbar and hoe,
I flattened hills.
I made mountains make valleys.
I banked back all of the sea this side.

Then turned into a bottomless bag, man,
I swallowed up all the sea-sound.
I saw I sucked in the force of the sea.

I lifted, man,
lifted up,
dropped off white bones like shell.

I climbed this high noon, man,
climbed this high noon,
hands sharp,
sharper than steel,
head big,
loaded with eyes.

I took this high noon, man,
took this high noon,
in claim of all earth,
in claim of all earth, man.

Just Being

I laughed and my echoes shook apples
off trees of a thousand lands

My swimming trailed one long lonely road
all deep in the sea

I stepped out and stood on a mountain top
high up in a sheet of sunlight

Going with All-Time Song

    Say
Goodmorning Love
in the midnight our market

    Say
Yesterday showed
our yearbook of yearning

Today washes
the words and eyes
in wonderment

    Say
Tomorrow is the torch focussed
now is my noontime

in the waking
   singing singing
I AM IN LOVE

Fantasy of an African Boy

Such a peculiar lot
we are, we people
without money, in daylong
yearlong sunlight, knowing
money is somewhere, somewhere.

Everybody says it's a big
bigger brain bother now,
money. Such millions and millions
of us don't manage at all
without it, like war going on.

And we can't eat it. Yet
without it our heads alone
stay big, as lots and lots do,
coming from nowhere joyful,
going nowhere happy.

We can't drink it up. Yet
without it we shrivel when small
and stop forever
where we stopped,
as lots and lots do.

We can't read money for books.
Yet without it we don't
read, don't write numbers,
don't open gates in other countries,
as lots and lots never do.

We can't use money to bandage
sores, can't pound it
to powder for sick eyes
and sick bellies. Yet without
it, flesh melts from our bones.

Such walled-round gentlemen
overseas minding money! Such
bigtime gentlemen, body guarded
because of too much respect
and too many wishes on them,

too many wishes, everywhere,
wanting them to let go
magic of money, and let it fly
away, everywhere, day and night,
just like dropped leaves in wind!

In God's Greatest Country, 1945

In this Lake Okeechobee land
of hibiscus, oranges and flamingos,
grass could deceive
it was sugarcane.

New like a city boy in
deep woods, I stood inside
the back of the bus, watching
empty seats in front
marked WHITES ONLY.

My friend sat, as any man sits
in a vacant public seat,
and the sun was attacked.
Horns grew in faces.

And the lady squirmed.
She yelled her person's purity
is blotted: a Black
violates her side.

Passions braked the bus.
The driver stood correctly,
legally, holding unholstered gun
coolly, like a Bible
to convert a Black.

'I'm British,' my friend said.
But under steel of eyes
there was a cooler confidence,
'Niggers are jes niggers.'

We stepped down between
fields of nodding sugarcane.
Pop-eyed, at the back of the bus,
with sheep caged faces,
the black Americans watched us go
across the country road.

In the free sunlight,
satisfying the other tribe,
we walked into the little
segregated town of Belleglade, Florida.

Notes on a Town on the Everglades, 1945

Sounds of 'Ma Baby Gone'
make the ghetto air in blues
in this Southern town.

It charges me with dread
with puzzlement with wonder
at this haunted mass of black people.

They hum the blues in shanty streets
and open fields. They dance the blues
in bars. They pray blues fashion.

They gesture and move and look
like refugees or campers on home ground,
or just a surplus of national propagation.

And fenced in, policed, blues-ridden,
the people plant wounds
on any close body it seems.

Women and men, all ages, go and come
in bandaged movements
like hospital escapees.

And on the compelling side,
the gleaming nearness of town,
the bridge is policing.

White men through their streets,
like white men in the fields,
are knowing and proud stalwarts.

With cold eyes like passionless gods
their groomed bodies go
extended with guns.

On an Afternoon Train from Purley to Victoria, 1955

Hello, she said and startled me.
Nice day. Nice day I agreed.
I am a Quaker she said and Sunday
I was moved in silence
to speak a poem loudly
for racial brotherhood.

I was thoughtful, then said
what poem came on like that?
One the moment inspired she said.
I was again thoughtful.

Inexplicably I saw
empty city streets lit dimly
in a day's first hours.
Alongside in darkness
was my father's big banana field.

Where are you from? she said.
Jamaica I said.
What part of Africa is Jamaica? she said.
Where Ireland is near Lapland I said.
Hard to see why you leave
such sunny country she said.
Snow falls elsewhere I said.
So sincere she was beautiful
as people sat down around us.

In-a Brixtan Markit

I walk in-a Brixtan markit,
believin I a respectable man,
you know. An wha happn?

Policeman come straight up
an search mi bag!
Man – straight to me.
Like them did a-wait fi me.
Come search mi bag, man.

Fi mi bag!
An wha them si in deh?
Two piece of yam, a dasheen,
a han a banana, a piece a pork
an mi lates Bob Marley.

Man all a suddn I feel
mi head nah fi me. This yah now
is when man kill somody, nah!

'Tony,' I sey, 'hol on. Hol on,
Tony. Dohn shove. Dohn shove.
Dohn move neidda fis, tongue
nor emotion. Battn down, Tony.
Battn down.' An, man, Tony win.

Two Black Labourers on a London Building Site

Been a train crash.
   Wha?
Yeh – tube crash.
   Who the driver?
Not a black man.
   Not a black man?
I check that firs.
   Thank Almighty God.
Bout thirty people dead.
   Thirty people dead?
Looks maybe more.
   Maybe more?
Maybe more.
   An black man didn drive?
No. Black man didn drive.

Stories by Bodyparts

1

I'm your breath-smell at waking.
I report your return from silence.
Use me in first kisses on children.
Use me in smiles on good-morning.

2

We are your eyes, your windows
on altitude and depth.
on faces hiding messages.
Sometimes we see
elevations unite levels.
Usually, horizons are fixed.
Blood boils us often
more than curved hips.
Bareness calls down hoods
yet you want to see the loving
next door: we wonder
what bird could be singing.
We wonder, to whom
could we expose we care.

3

We are your feet. We rubbed
away your baby tantrums
into leg-shapes of clockhands.
We stand at doorways:
no last abode anywhere.
Obsessed with wings, you make us
go about in traps.
We climb we fall.
We linger it hurts.
If you laugh or kiss, always
we are way at the end.
We dash for the bus, your
destination's eyes, high up
at its rear, laugh at us
and disappear. Then at last

we face outwards, like
clothes-irons rested
going colder and colder.
We see: no bath was ever able
to soak away our travels.

4

I am your hand. I hang
lightly or become a stone.
Agent of eyes and heart
I pull triggers.
I stroke up love.
I wrap up weapon.
Good cash or bad or its absence,
all arrive for pocketing.
And as this ladling palm, I take
a nail driven through me.
But like a leaf, I wave,
I shiver,
I shrivel,
I slip away.

I am Racism

I am the progress of tribalism.
I am civilised. I well know
the fixations of nonspecials.
I must protect pure and sane futures
and keep myself well walled.
You see I do deserve
the switch I press in others.
    After all I am Racism.

I am the magic embodied before all eyes.
I am the most beautiful. I am
offended when nonspecials get seen
as my equal, since I already know
an ethnic difference is the sign
of nonspecial people. After all
I carry the supreme essence.
I have a position to uphold.
And I well know I am extolled
in secret by nonspecials.
You see I do deserve special rights.
    After all I am Racism.

I am a royal household.
I live in an exclusive range.
Success of my special difference
displays me worldwide. And since
I have the ways to win, it helps
to underline the obvious.
You see I do deserve
the core of any country.
    After all I am Racism.

I am the marbled column holding up
the sky. I must control to keep
entrusted gifts. I must wipe out
any sign to remove me, particularly
a sign from any nonspecial.
You see I do deserve the strength
I get reinforcements from.
    After all I am Racism.

I am the church.
I must show how God is one-faced.
I am university.
I must show how to disguise
one dominance is absolute.
I am prime minister.
I must show how I keep my word
and defend goodness of my supporters
I am the press.
I must recycle the people's confectionery.
I am the police.
I must bend laws in my defence.
You see I do deserve my slow
as well as my quick wits.
    After all I am Racism.

    I am the noontime in night-time
the unique self, operated
in truth and trust. I'll be spoilt
if I change. I must defend to keep
the special success I am.
You see I do deserve
most wealth and ways and means.
After all I am Racism.

New World Colonial Child

I arrive to doubtful connections,
to questionable paths,
to faces with obscure
disclosures, with reticent
voices, not clear why
my area is inaccessible,
my officials are not promoters.

Odd farthings drive the circles
bare, around the houses, like
goats tethered and forgotten.

I can't endure like my father.
I wait bowed. I wait
in rain-saturation,
in sunlight-dazzle.

Dark valleys and snow domes
are elsewhere. I am a piece
of disused gold mine, sometimes
a feather of shot game, other
times a seedbed of obsessions.

And making it is making.
Who isn't faced
to surrender money or knowhow,
surrender strength or bold,
reluctant or benevolent blood?

In the haughty handling
winners keep a military stance.
Avenues were never landscaped
for people blueprinted for rags.

A meeting has stayed
on a footing of war,
levels of weaponry unknown:
words misstate manoeuvres.
I hide. I admit
at best I am stubborn
like weeds on a path.

Absence of a choice has
a grasp of a slow death.
Absence of a hero makes men
headless, makes world-successes
work from failed retaliation,
And who shall expose
the virtues of difference?

Father's learning long taught
him, he's too lazy
to be man, too worthless
to be paid for work. He walks
like a loaded donkey,
unqualified to engage
essential listener. He knows
knowledge inflates a person
beyond little speeches in fragments.

I cannot assess my father.
I do not know what makes him
history. He's merely our
mystery of helplessness,
our languagemaster dumb
with forgetfulness, our
captain without compass.

And I cannot fathom
the people he's given me.
I still have to see if
our failures opened
inner doors of a meeting,
behind netting jaws, more firmly
than pain or profit.

I do not know my kinspeople
to be less than I know them,
yet judgements make me
feel they are less.

I do not know my losses,
I only sense them. I
do not know any licence
against me, it only seems so.
But a rope at my neck is
a shame I am born in
that I can't understand.

I hold on to a pride:
I own a map
underfoot. I own a king
and kingdom and robes
and rites I use.

On May 24 every year
I march, in fresh khaki shorts.
We wave the flag. I
with my slave scars march
and sing: Britons never,
never, shall be slaves.

In my dumbness I know
in our sky-wide gestures
gentle strengths arouse
a light in everyone.
How can I say what best
my heritage surrendered?

How can I know my voice
isn't the grunt of a pig,
isn't the squawking of a goose,
or the howling of wind?

A colony is a lair
of a country found. New lords
give names to people and places
and things and stamp them.
Equal terms would hold
a more-than-equal people
to a gunless robbery.

A colony has no resource
value for itself. A colony
never redeems itself with payment,
it merely receives.

A colony is given freedom,
when freedom has always been there.
A colony is given
Independence, when independence
can only be arrested.

Without plan or invitation,
like a season impels
I am charged to move.

I leave the encampment.
Like fresh awakening
I emerge round corners.
And again a different
weather is fierce
and I freeze-burn.

How shall anyone agree
a colony-native isn't
a colonised ghetto captive?
How shall we
clear away old orders?

Island Man

How I have watched you chop and ruffle
a tired face of land with hands
like dead roots, at full life
keeping back weeds
from a hillside patch.

How I see winds molest
your rags rotten with sweat,
see the sun paint you deeper and deeper
and suck your bosom dry.

Man grilled in sunken eyes,
minder of bush knowledge
the wind laughs at repeatedly,
knocking down your sticks,
beating up your few hills of yam,
I have watched you, seen you
stumble to shadows
reckoning insensibly
the season's and land's potential.

A new and clean voice burdens you:
your eyes hide from the meeting,
your humbled smile trembles with fear,
your arms are restless
like wild wings of a seized bird.

Unable to go any other way,
object of a landscape,
you lift weighted feet
with the memory of chains
in floods and arid ground:
your shoulder rocks a dirty bag,
your stumpy machete in your grasp.

Between bamboos and old palmtrees
you are in pursuit,
making me know I see a man
loaded in mind, but only
with the ways of his woods
that exclude him
and control him by compulsive tracks,
by strong sunrise
and its last rage of departure.

Luckless man of ceaseless attempts,
I have known you and watched you.
I watch you closer
now, watching myself.

It's Me Man

I wouldn't be raven
    though dressed so
I wouldn't bleed my last
    though crushed
I wouldn't stay down
    though battered
I wouldn't be convinced
    though worst man
I wouldn't stay pieces
    though dissected
I wouldn't wear the crown
    though king of rubbish
I wouldn't stay dead
    though killed
I wouldn't stay dead
    though killed

Great Story

He drops out of sunlight,
voice like velvet, clean, unhurried,
says he's GREAT.

What makes GREAT, John asks him.
Knowhow, GREAT says.
Proof is the guts of GREAT.

His friends fall out of leaves.
More friends leap out of grass.
They burn John's house in a flaring fire.

John stands, unbelieving,
See? GREAT says. See change
in bricks to ashes.

See clean-up of fusion,
combustive excitement,
so well futuristic?

And there's more, GREAT says.
GREAT'S friends draw close to John.
GREAT'S friends hold John.

They break John's spine.
They crack John's skull.
They break John's legs and arms.

GREAT works on John.
GREAT works on a reputation.
Skills of GREAT rebuild John.

Reporters flock in with cameramen.
JOHN WALKS. JOHN IS REPAIRED.
O the extra excellence of GREAT.

The world is elated.
Relief absorbs the world.
The world enjoys relief.

Confession

I had a condition, she said.
I was born in England, you see.
Till last week, I was seventeen
years old. I've never seen
a Caribbean island, where my parents
came from. But I was born to know
black people had nothing. Black people
couldn't run their own countries,
couldn't take part in running the world.
Black people couldn't even run
a good two-people relationship.
They couldn't feed themselves, couldn't
make money, couldn't pass exams
and couldn't keep the law. And
black people couldn't get awards
on television. I asked my mother
why black people never achieved,
never explored, always got charity.
My mother said black people were cursed.
I knew.
I knew that.
I knew black people were cursed.
And I was one.
All the time I knew I was cursed.
Then going through a book on art
one night, a painting showed me
other people in struggle.
It showed me a different people like that.
Ragged, barefoot, hungry looking
they were in struggle.
I looked up.
The people needed: other people needed.
Or needed to remember their struggle.
Or even just to know
their need of struggle.
No. Not cursed.
Black people were not cursed.

Benediction

Thanks to the ear
that someone may hear

Thanks to seeing
that someone may see

Thanks to feeling
that someone may feel

Thanks to touch
that one may be touched

Thanks to flowering of white moon
and spreading shawl of black night
holding villages and cities together.

Thinking Back on Yard Time

We swim in the mooneye.
The girls' brown breasts float.
Sea sways against sandbanks.

We all frogkick water.
Palm trees stand there watching
with limbs dark like our crowd.

We porpoise-dive, we rise,
we dog-shake water from our heads.
Somebody swims on somebody.

We laugh, we dry ourselves.
Sea-rolling makes thunder
around coast walls of cliffs.

Noise at Square is rum-talk
from the sweaty rum bar
without one woman's word.

Skylarking, in our seizure,
in youthful bantering,
we are lost in togetherness.

Our road isn't dark tonight.
Trees – mango, breadfruit – all,
only make own shapely shadow.

Moon lights up pastureland.
Cows, jackass, all, graze quietly.
We are the cackling party.

Memory

Dawn hangs a crimson dusk
of all the Flame Trees in bloom
with all the hibiscus. Bare feet go
collecting animals in heavy dew.

Morning delivers new sun.
Smoke rises from little kitchens.
Every passing person calls out
'Good morning!'

Eyes go drowsy in blazing afternoon.
Golden wasps shimmer.
Clothes collect summer smells.

Swift brown bats litter dusk.
Anancy weaves in log cottages.
Grandma's knowing ripens.

Night ferments mango-walk.
The caring night pouches
busy sea and static hills
together with flatland palm trees.

Anancy: spider hero of Caribbean folk tales.

Nana Krishie the Midwife

So keen on me those old eyes
the tracked black face
flowed with light

The tongue and gum ladled
stubborn words remembering
how I the boy child had knocked
thirty years before and hustled her
to come to the little cottage

Come with owl's wisdom and red
calico bag of tricks
to end labour: snap
and smack a newborn to cry

And now she looked at me surprised
and not at all surprised I had
come back from abroad
looking in a widened range
out of miracles she used and knew
time had discredited

For her ancestor's knack
her tabooed secrets now worked
in books of others
as ancient practices

Dreaming in her illiterate life
I felt the faltering tones
her startling shivered voice
thanking God
for showing me ever so well

Reclamation

Suspended and choiceless
I grew in abeyance.
Memories mocked me.

Old sun-scented beds were haunted
realms, of gestures unfinished.
My path was a tunnel
ending into nighttime.

Nature obeyed no black man:
all the lands, oceans and space.

Black men swapped gold for trinkets.
They played hide-and-seek with ghosts
and raised up dust for rain.

Yet there was a knowing I was
marooned from. And I didn't
know what or how or why.
My sanctuary held no truth
for I could not enter it.

Voices in me grew beyond me.
Voices in me grew to pentecostal bedlam.
I knew I must retrace a travel.

I knew I must go back
through groans and griefs
through putrefaction
through shit of ships' bowels
through staring eyes and tears unwept.

I must go back through a march from home
through graves at sea without goodbye.
I must go back
through friendless arrivals
through beautiful bewildering faces
through change of name
through loss of tongue
through loss of face
through exclusion and sweating

for mountains of money
to the grave of a slave
through people fixed in a ship like wood
in long listless days and days
over the swells of indifferent seas.

I must absorb you
Middle Passage,
must refine you, must
distil a journey, like any,
into an innocent voice.

Here I am.
Here I am, where
at beginning one sun
daubed and brushed me
in silence, and I became
obsessed lover of the dance.

And here are these eyes.
All unfathomable eyes surround me
in motherland.

Unreachable time has turned
familiar voices strange,
but kept every face my own.
And none is my grandmother.
None is my grandfather.
None is my known cousin.

But called or uncalled, these are names
that are musical instruments
that announce death and life,
announce trespasses and hauntings,
announce a welcome and redemption.

Reinitiate,
rededicate,
o all of me,
all of our dead
dumped at sea unloved,
and those given the destination
to a life they never owned.

Approach me.
Approach me
drums, whistles, chants.
Approach me.
Reconsecrate the days that carry me.

I hear riddles.
I hear proverbs
mixed in drumbeat.
I hear the time of day-one.

Exorcise me.
Exorcise a castaway
in hypnotic rites.

I am a sacred place.
I am the beginning of my ancestors.
I open the way as first and close it as last,
I am a flaming stone.
I am a tree never to be cut
and a word reserved for ceremony.

My tongue chisels and
my tongue churns old words. I'm
rolled back from sand like ocean waves
that rise to begin again.
I sing an old song like a first song.

Release is an unworded pledge.
Impulses poise my body.

We dance.
We dance in dust.
We dance. We dance. We dance.

With found faces and drumming,
with found faces and drumming
I'm new spirit out of skin.

I'm new spirit out of skin,
with found faces and drumming...

Goodmornin Brodda Rasta

Good-days wash yu mi brodda
a-mek peace possess yu
an love enlightn yu
a-mek yu givin be good
an yu evermore be everybody
a-mek Allness affec yu always
an yu meetn of eye to eye be vision
an all yu word dem be word of wondament

Approach and Response

Now you have excited her.
You have started the sound
of the abrasive wheel:
that heart, so tightly tied
with pain and tucked away.

You are still far far
from a welcome touch in this house
and the one chair that holds
a wispy woman through
most nights. But you are
guilty of arousal.

You have knocked a door.
You have shaken up death again.
You have rattled account demands
impossible to settle.

Thinkin Loud-Loud

Yu sen fo we to Englan, she sey.
Yu buy de house.
Yu buy de car.
We inside dohn roll fo food.
I expectin yu numba 6 child.
Why yu beatin out yu brain on books
wha tight like a rockstone?
Find teacher. Find teacher, she sey.

Gal, I sey, fifty year I walkin earth:
ow can I mek a teacher wise
ABC still a-puzzle me?
Ow can I show we own boy an girl dem
words on me eye put up high wall?

She sey, yu sign yu name wid X.
Yu show no paperwork, but
yu av yu workins
wid pencil an paper in yu head.

Gal, I sey, dat worded page
is a spread of dead tings: insect dem
wha stares at me
doing notn sayin notn
but turn dark night
an bodda me an bodda me
fo dat time I hear print a-talk
like voices of we children.

Calabash Tree

You drew me to come
to you. Calabash Tree,
short trunked with long and leafy whips
at foothills here in the bush.

Your shape is
a confusion of fountain jets:
your lines make
an extraordinary wild face.

Your loose open top receives draperies
of sunlight.
I move and rub
your thin flakes of bark.

I climb up easily and sit: I know
streaked with purple your blooms
of yellow surprise with stink.

Scattered on the network of branches
or stuck to your trunk
green fruits are solitary.

On the ground some are rotting skulls.
And tied young they would have flowed
into pearshape
or oblong or other forms
for maracas, water gourds, ornaments.

You make me wonder.
You let it known your parts are fibred
for ribs of boats, tool handles,
cattle yokes or saddle trees.

Did you start out to surrender
at arrival, to become scattered
pieces, on the sea, in men's hands
and backs of animals?

I wonder.
I wonder how you first
received your impetus
to show the sun
its transformation.

The Coming of Yams and Mangoes and Mountain Honey

Handfuls hold hidden sunset
stuffing up bags
and filling up the London baskets.
Caribbean hills have moved and come.

Sun's alphabet drops out of branches.
Coconuts are big brown Os,
pimentoberries little ones.
Open up papaw like pumpkin you get
the brightness of macaw.

Breadfruit a green football,
congo-peas like tawny pearls,
mango soaked in sunrise,
avocado is a fleshy green.

Colours of sun, stalled in groups,
make market a busy meeting.
The sweetnesses of summer settle smells.

Mints and onions quarrel.
Nutmeg and orange and cinnamon hug
themselves in sun-perfume.

Some of the round bodies shown off
have grown into long shapes.
Others grew fisty and knobbled.
Jars hold black molasses like honey.

And yams the loaves
of earth's big bellies and sun,
plantains too huge to be bananas,
melons too smooth to be pineapples –
chocho, okra, sweetsop, soursop, sorrel –
all are sun flavoured geniuses.

Nights once lit the growing lots
with fields of squinting kitibus.
Winds polished some of the skins cool but warm
when sun drew stripes on fish.

But, here, you won't have a topseat cooing
in peppers, won't hear the nightingale's
notes mixed with lime juice.

Red buses pass for donkeys now.
Posters of pop stars hang by.

Caribbean hills have moved
and come to London
with whole words of the elements.
Just take them and give them
to children, to parents and the old folks.

kitibu: the click-beetle, or firefly, with two luminous spots
that squint light in the dark.

FROM

Hot Earth Cold Earth

(1995)

Spirits of Movement

Surely, so alike, airborne wind gave birth
to water, issued the denser wash
and earthed the early offspring.

Inbuilt is wind-inheritance.
Rage of leaves resists face-wash
it is wind's arrival in trees.

Hear sea waves work-choir,
hear any waterfall wonder,
its temple-roar of wind flooding woods.

A restless transparent busyness
going and going. Spirits of movement.
Both break all shores, mad mad in search.

Wind plays wild bands of ghosts.
Water organises running river
and drives rain-floods hustling.

On any sitting duty
like being a pond or puddle,
canal or glassful

water waits to run away
or just disappear like wind.
In a settled state water is sad.

Drop a stone in a sleepy pool
you hear the sulk
of static water voiced.

Lock up water, give it time, it'll leave.
Drink it down, it presses wanting exit.
A job done, water vanishes.

Water'll freshen any body part
and be ready, hanging
in drips, to be off.

Does its work, yes. But to be
ungraspable, like wind,
water insists on its transfiguration.

Haiku Moments: 1

1

The sea-sound sunlight –
pinnate leaves of palms rattle
a lost young bird cries.

2

The humming bird sucks
the open red hibiscus
fluttering its leaves.

3

Hill tree staged parrots
woodpecker screams in the noon
stream pours into self.

4

The frogs are croaking
fireflies wink together
darkness drips rainfall.

Hot Day Before My Time

Scent of blossom
scent of blossom them have tipsy bees a-dawdle,
sun face a-drip it dazzle.
Collect hot earth creation them from sunhot:
bag them up, bag up a nation market lot.

Mortar pound
mortar pound roast coffee
like cassava fo bammy,
cocobeans fo chocolate,
corn fo cornpone
and make dog ketch a bone.

Mango a-ripe, mango a-ripe,
bird them in a branch full a fight.
Breadfruit fatten up cut hog,
spiced pork sizzle fo dogwood log.

Hen lay egg, hen a-cackle:
mongoose know whey to get a suckle.
A banana-day, man, a banana pay
come bubble up in a rum day.

cut hog: castrated pig.

Afternoon Sunhot

Watch palm trees they swing
blue sky red hibiscus
in strangle of twigs and vines

and the stream cool
hardly a-gargle
speckled sun buttons

and birds
never did care –
jus a-whistle
and sing

mongoose a-prowlin hard
a-look and shriek fo blood

My Arrival

Showing the creature I landed
I slipped from my mother's womb
flesh connected, laced in a blood-spatter.

My father waited with a bottle of rum.
The moon floated somewhere.
The sea drummed and drummed our coastline.
Mullets darted in wooded streams.

A good night to end labour – Saturday.
The country-midwife held me up,
'Look. Is yu third boy child!'
My mother asked, 'Him all right?'

'Yes – all eyes, all ears.
Yes – all hands, all feet.'
My mother whispered, 'Thank God.'
My granny said, 'My Jim-Jim.
My husband! You come back?'

I slept.
Roosters crowed
all around the village.

In the sun's hot eye
my umbilical cord was dressed
with wood ash, castor oil and nutmeg
and buried under a banana-sucker.
There, a tree made fruits, all mine.

Haiku Moments: 2

5

New baldheaded glow
again, skyline-face, you start
your old round of climb.

6

Cocks chase gathered hens
Village pigs all squeal for feed –
another sunrise,

7

Smells of brewed coffee,
sprats frying up, yams roasted –
soon, church bell for school.

8

Going, dog leads man,
man rides the donkey slowly
leading the white goat.

My Cousin Rosetta

The river washed her breasts,
trees dressed her with beads:
she sits encamped behind the hill.

In her hut, she looks in
the broken and speckled mirror
and sees her face
weather-worked, unrouged,
and hair tangled, fibre stubborn
like a pile of coconut coir.

Dismayed, she dreams of how
and how she might conform
with trends she sees in town.

She has tried.
The pink powder she patted on
mismatched the brown of ther face.

She sits down, discontent
with a body dawn-dusky, longing
to be styled on world highstreets
in all O all that is newest.

Early Days Thinking Is Only So Much

I didn't think I shouldn't be hungry
I didn't think of government
I didn't blame my father's husbandry
everything was just as it was

I didn't think a bellyful
of nothing was nothing
I didn't think I didn't deserve nothing
when there was food
there was everything
and there was a lot I knew

I knew we should bow
to the well-rounded people
bow to the best educated people
bow to the whitest faces
go to school breakfast or not
and that was just how it was
and that would have to be right

Our everyday business was havenots' business
and we worked and joked and played games
and laughed often as we could

And fruit-season or famine
or flood-time or drytime
everything was just as it was

And I didn't think that anything
was wrong or anything was right
that education and knowhow should be
a mystery like witchcraft

It was just as it was
and everything would have to be right

Bluefoot Traveller

Man
  who the hell is you?
What hole you drag from
  and follah railway line
  pass plenty settlement
  sleep under trees
  eat dry bread and water
  sweat like a carthorse
  to come and put body
  and bundle down in we village?
How we to feel you not obeah-man
  t'ief
  Judas with lice
  and a dirty mout?
Why you stop here? Get news
  Mericans open up dollar place
  in we districk?
Here we got woman givin away
  to follah-line man –
  and water an donkey and lan?
Bluefoot
  I considerin you hard hard
I point out to you –
  move!
It in my bones deep deep –
  pick up possessions
  walk again
An you don't call out
  a battalion of fists
  don't pull down
  hills of rockstone
  don't bring out
  woods of lickle bumpy sticks
  to drop on your head-top
  an crack it up.

obeah-man: witchcraft man.

Faces Around My Father

Hunger stormed my arrival.
I arrived needing.
I had need of older selves.
My mother's milk met
my parching. Streams were here
like stars and stones,
and a fatherhood compelling.

Fatherhood tailed a line
of fathers, we knew: a prehistory
book, a full season open all time,
a storehouse for emptying
for renewal, a marketing
of strength that stuffs away
richness of summers upon summers.

I'd work up a clean slate full.
Crafts and arts would engage me,
my urgent hands would grow
in homely voices,
the land would amaze
my roaming eyes,
incite my impulses.

Head striped, sir, with sounds
of birds in the hills,
sweat smells in clothes stuck
with soil and sun, you come
into the house at evening
like a piece of hillside.
I wait to take your drinking mug.

A silence surrounds your eating.
The dog catches and gulps
pieces of food you pitch
that somehow cut your distance.
A son washes your feet.
Another brings glowing firewood:
you light up your pipe.

Your incidental money getting
not believed, a child asks for cash
for boots or book.
Our words are stones
tossed on a genial guest.
You vanish into twilight.
A sleeping house receives you back.

And father is a scripture
lesson. Father knows
blueprints of seeds in the moon,
knows place of a cockerel's
testicles, knows coins
in minutes. His body sets
defences, sets boundaries.

Yet strong hints had soaked us:
we are not beautiful,
we are a cancellation
of abundance and sharing.
I am charged with unmanageable
hunger. I am trumpeted
for ungettable distances.

I must cross our moat of sea,
and I have no way. I must list
lost tracks, must write
my scanning of time, must plant
hot words in ministers like cool
communion bread. Yet I should drown
in language of our lanes.

In and about your preclusion, sir,
dead footsteps entrapped me.
You chopped wood and sang,
I listened behind a wall.
In hot field of pineapples
fermenting, I watched you
dreaming: I walked away.

Your tool's edge touched work
barely, and you resharpened.
Sir, in fresh sunny magnitude,
your dramatic grind of machete
should flatten forests. Yet
you left for work looking,
'What boss shall I serve today?'

Were you being your father
or just a loser's son? Sir,
did old scars warn you to yield
and hide? Were you strangely
full of a friendly enemy
voice? Did you feel
your movements failure-fixed?

Schemed in your steady
good health, we were placed
to proliferate loneliness,
birthdays of lacks,
trouble growing in our flesh,
lips moved by ventriloquists,
beginnings with approaches of daggers.

We needed that safety, sir,
that wonderment of caressing eye,
that steadiness that allows
strongest and sweetest voice,
that sanctioned contentment
that walked bright
in the constellation of children.

Our voices deepened,
our limbs emulated trees,
our appetites expanded,
our silence encircled you
like strangers with killer plans.
I disowned you to come to know
thanks to connection that someone may feel.

I saw your body full
and fit and free, ready
in the sun's recycle,
ever the husbandman
of exalted acclamations.
I saw you die, sir,
well bluffed by subjugation.

Folk Proverbs Found Poems

1

Stump-a-foot man can't kick
with his good foot.

2

Tiger wants to eat a child, tiger says
he could swear it was a puss.

3

Is a blessing me come me see you:
eye-to-eye joy is a love.

4

Is better to walk for nothing
than sit down for so-so.

5

A man with half-a-foot
must dance near his door.

6

Good-friend you can't buy.
Cheap bargain takes money.

7

Better go heaven a pauper
than go hell a rector.

8

If ants waller too much in fat,
fat will drown ants.

9

Stretch your hand and give
it's a God own grace.

stump-a-foot: stumpy or one-legged.

In Our Year 1941 My Letter to You Mother Africa

                I sit
        under the mango tree in our yard.
        A woman passes along the village road,
        loaded like a donkey.
                        I remember
I start my seventeenth year today
full of myself, but worried, and sad
remembering, you sold my ancestors
labelled, *not for human rights,*
And, O, your non-rights terms were
the fire of hell that stuck.
                        Mother Africa
my space walks your face
and I am condemned.
I refuse to grow up fixed here
going on with plantation lacks
and that lack of selfhood. Easily
I could grow up all drastic and extreme
and be wasted by law.
I want a university in me as I grow.

        And now
        three village men pass together,
        each gripping his plantation machete.
                        I remember
we are stuck in time and hidden.
I refuse to be stuck in a maze
gripping a plantation machete.
l refuse to be Estate 'chop-bush' man
and a poverty path scarecrow.
Refuse to live in the terror of floods
and drought, and live left-out and moneyless.
I refuse to worry-worry Jesus Christ
with tear-faced complaints. And, O, I refuse
to walk my father's deadness,
schooled to be wasted lawfully
and refuse it
I am doubly doomed to be wasted by law,

Mother Africa
New World offices and yards of rejection
threaten me, like every shack dweller seared
by poverty and feels disgraced.
And people positioned to make changes
are not bothered how poverty sinks in.
Help stop my vexed feelings growing.
Help me have a university in me.

And now
a banana-truck passes.
I remember
I dread that cap-in-hand
my father. His selfhood gutted –
all seasoned plantation corned-pork –
no education habit is there.
Not seeing his need and his rights
to help make the world free,
not seeing the club of countries
that confiscated his ancestors' lives
still set his boundaries, not seeing
no god for our good with us,
my father demands no more
than a small cut of land, hidden.
Mother Africa
nobody at home here has any
education habit. Nobody stirs differently.
And I want life of the world in print.
I want to move about in all ages.
Not stay deformed, arrested, driven
by any drillmaster's voice telling
the growing good of myself is cancelled.
I want to be healed of smashed-up selfhood,
healed of the beating-up by bad-man history.
I want a university in me as a man.

And now
children pass by, going to loiter
around the tourist beach.
I remember
you were pillaged easily
and gutted easily. Existing dumb

you lost your continental wealth,
our inheritance, my inheritance.
And, a settled absence, you are a fixed
nonparticipator I never see. And while
others come and go from their motherlands,
I live marooned, renamed 'Negro'
meaning, of no origin,
not eligible for human rights.
                              Mother Africa
I walk your face
and my heritage is pain.
And there somewhere
you make not one move.
Say nothing. Do nothing.
And I feel excessive doings could grip me.
I could call on bad doings as normal
and be wasted by law.
I want a university in me.

        And now
        at our gate, a village beggar stands
        calling my mother.
                          I remember
I am third generation since slavery,
born into people stricken in traps,
Eight generations departed
with a last sigh, aware they leave
offsprings all heirs to losses,
to nothing, to a shame, and to faces
who meet enmity in the offices
of their land and the world.
You say nothing, do nothing
while your bosom's gold and gems are stars
in other people's days
around the world. And scattered
stubbornly, we are here
in the sun's comings and goings
anguished for our human status back.
                          Mother Africa
do you know, cruelties of your lacks
join forces with New World mangling?
Now I want to be healed.
I want university.

And now
village voices go by
strong with the adjective 'black'
in their curses.
                    I remember
in lessons at school you were degraded.
No village man accepts his photographs
that printed him truly black.
You never made a contact
never inspired me
never nurtured, counselled or consoled me.
I have never seen you, Africa,
never seen your sights or heard your sounds,
never heard your voice at home,
never understood one common
family thing about you beneath
one crinkly head or naked breast.
Any wonder I have no love for you?
Any wonder everybody at school despised you?
Tradition has it, our people's travel
to you does not happen. Visits
to a motherland are overlords' privilege.
What is your privilege?
                    Mother Africa
I want university.
Is there any help in you?
Will I have to store,
or bag-up and walk with, inherited hurt
and outrage of enslavement?
Will I transcend it?
Or will I grow up wasted
in deformity or being outlaw?

Lion

Body colour of hay, big cat.
Staring face a fearless look.
A superstar nature presents,
getting featured more
than eagles flying and whales swimming.

Hunger switches you on, big cat.
Padded toe-walk breaks
into trots, into athletic dash.
You flash claw–daggers and crusher–jaws
to hug a zebra
and kiss and cap the nose and mouth.
O what a love for flesh!
What a stunning show, devouring
someone different at only contact!

Vermin and flies choose you, big cat.
Night sky carries your quaking roars
in company with fellow lions only.

Your beauty, your strength, your success
fix you with a dread
of your devouring.
Do creatures like you ever feel
a hollow of helpless loneliness?

What Is No Good?

I will stop
night's return,
stop dawn, stop dusk,
leave your eyes on
white dazzle of noon.

I will let sea rocks move
and fill in dark depths of oceans,
let storm clouds
and November be whitened,
leave you the glitter of space.

I will wash out
the brown of earth,
bleach out the tarmac of roads,
let gardens be white roses only,
leave you brilliant desert ways.

Sunlight's tanning
I will cancel,
leave you the show
of a tree
newly stripped of bark.

I will leave you time
with a dazzling face,
leave you a pale pale red
fixed on each other.
Would absence be abundance?

Ol Style Freedom

        Darlin mi darlin
you lying down
all legs belly bosom face
quiet-quiet in room here
All of all so much –
street poverty can't touch me now
Hurts – threats – banished away

No pockets on me
   I a millionaire
No test before me to fail me
   I know I know everything

        Darlin mi darlin
you the offerin with all things
   all of all so much
every tick of clock stopped
every traffic groan switched off
every peep of bird shut up
only sea waves risin risin

        Hope she fixed sheself fo no-baby
            fixed sheself fo no-baby
I in a king time king time king time
   king time
      king time
         king time...

I Am on Trial After Being Juror on a Black Man

Fear, don't trouble me, don't
drag me down. I'll look around
this court and not surrender.
I mus burst up the bite
of knife-edge words.
I mus fence miself with fists.

All the same another
doomsday. Another time
of trapped feet walled up.

Another lot of captors.
Robots encircle me
with power of law
in priest robes,
in robes of angels
and the uniform
of the blue clothes gang.

Man, take it. Take it
man! At sweetest we attack.
We get each other or plan
it. And I am caught,
noosed, because I survive;
because I move where I belong
and dance my survival.

Always my backing is weak.
But I won't break up, before
eyes of knowhow
as my people always fall,
sharing majesty of a room
watching swirls of robes,
victims in a classic show.

I wasn't born to satisfy
the skills of robots.
I wasn't born to be bullseye.

I was born because
I was born
like tree and bird and star.
Tomorrow, I must get away.

A man must feel his woman's leg.
A man mustn't fight,
fight, fight between trees,
between walls
between lamposts
to have a sightless moment
overshadow him like a net.

I wasn't born to be turned
into outlaw. I was
born like everyone,
with different fingerprints
and a different face
and have to find my way
through everybody.
And I have to find my way.

I look at the jury.
See me push back a giggle,
for jackass,
their little black juror:
man drilled to kill he smile.

See the robots whisper,
like lovebirds, for me
to see them as gods.
And let them toss about
questions about me. Let them
play ping-pong with my life
and movements.

They can never know
I can't agree. I can't agree
I was born a failure. I can't
agree I was born disqualified.

I can't agree I was born
the material for robots to pulp
into their successes.

They can never know I was born
because a man must
fight back, and not
accept the role of dirt.
Them wi neva see I mus add-to
an add-to all mi weakness them
or find strength of a storm.

Hitting back keeps everybody
absorbed, keeps me
with a big backlog
of moves to make up.

And they will hurt me well.
And they will know they please
everybody. And they will watch
to see if I rise. And I
will rise, at hours and places
in unexpected ways.

And my face changes
as I've never known it.
And I don't laugh, over
the people I make mourn,
and make me mourn, like my
accomplices here in robes.

And they dangle me
on rope-ends of words.
They focus robot faces
on me, like a squad of gunmen.
They toy with my life.

And no more an apology
I can't hide my eyes.
No more a repentant rubbish
a man must eat and wear
and drink and dance.

A man must show:
I made it
I take
I win
I have. I have!
And they'll hide him away
as a maniac, knowing they have
all the holy, legal, regal connections.

And I unfocus my eyes.
My answers are merely
No and Yes.

And I remember. I remember,
the blue clothes gang came at me:
    How many white women you fucked?
    How many how many how many?
    How old how middle-aged how young?

I give no answer. Because
I give no answer, I get a blow
for every white woman I bedded,
they said, and every one
I wished to bed. I cried out
cried out cried out and said:
    Black women are not mine.
    Black women are not mine to keep.
    Can't you make friends?
    Is that why you punish me?

I am the object of the smokescreen
ceremony. I must speak
when spoken to. My answers
again are No and Yes.

The switches of robots spark
each other. I'm worthless, they say.
Everything I have is worthless.
I should be dumped
away from people
away from animals
away from God.

Yet when I stood here
for suspicious loitering
was it for that?
When I stood here
for removing goods
was it for that?
When I stood here
for stripping old people of money
was it for that?
When I stood here
for wounding, as I stand
here now, wasn't I wounded?

Thoughts Going Home

Twelve years of darkness and sea
between me and the village house
I ventured from, so far.

What lifetime hopes go back
with me? What disappointments?
What discoveries from eye to eye?

And seeing is now your fingers' edge
on shapes. And sounds defined keenly.
I will be a voice. Your son –
strange words with foreign airs.
And a full body – a change
from scarce and slender times.

How are you without sturdy legs
that firmly took sharp sunny hills
and wielded hoe, machete, axe,
and carried baskets of yams,
carried bundles of wood, across
muddy tracks and the rough lowlands?

How are you with slow searching
feet and empty eyes? How is it
alone, in a cave of night
continuously? Are we little ones
who engage you or lost men
whose return you await?

So much awakening never touched you.
But, mother, I have seen best educated
men, centrally celebrated men,
whose words to me showed their eyes
to be a day-old kitten.

A bright moon, it will be.
Shadows unknown sitting about.
Dim lamps on bare shelves.
Everybody asleep, guarded by uprights.

Will father glide in tonight?
Through the plain walls of cedar
he so loved? Or be a swift man-size
feather, down the rafter-ceiling?

Will I know the hibiscus road?
With my broken steps, will I find
the cottage that cradles home
with the old one waiting?

A Schooled Fatherhood

There in my small-boy years that day
couldn't believe the shock,
the blow that undid me, seeing him abused,
reduced, suddenly. Helpless, without honour
without respect, he stood indistinct,
called 'boy' by the white child
in the parents' look-away, 'don't-care' faces.
Lost, in a peculiar smile – being
an error, a denial of the man I copied,
that big-big man I'm one day to be – he made
a black history I didn't know swamp me,
hurt me, terror-hands of a dreaded ghost.

Two men apart, from now – with him
not able to see, not able
to keep pace with time or know
my secret eye watchful –
I began to see
educated voices charging his guts
like invisible pellets of a gun
imbedding *in him*, daytime, nighttime.
And soon, he clean forgot
who he was. Then with his roots
and person's rights wiped away
he knew he'd known nothing always.
His deep man-structure dismantled,
a tamed dog came in him and gave him face
gave him readiness for his job –
delivering shot birds between his teeth
to get a patting beside high boots –
    my father
      my first lord
        my inviolable king.

Countryman O

Countryman O
wha happn then wha happn?

Me come a Kingston town
to look aroun
to look aroun me spend
mi only pound.

Countryman O
wha happn then wha happn?

Me come a Kingston town
to buy a yard a cloth
to buy a yard a cloth
me find mi money short,
Me find me buy one rum
and all money drink down.

Countryman O
wha happn then wha happn?

Friend and me had a row.
Meet up with him jus now
and say, 'Off you knees
with you *sorry* and *please*.
Like a decent bar bum
always the best of chum,
jus say to the barman:
'Give you friend halfbottle a rum.'

Countryman O
wha happn then wha happn?

Back Home Weddn Speech

Man-eye go and fall on woman
man-skin catch a-fire.
Woman say, 'Is me – why you on fire.'

Woman-eye go and fall on man
woman-skin flutter like storm.
Man say, 'Is me – why you born.'

Man-dread say, 'Oh! I gone and get
long belly horse
and must feed it like a good-cause!'
Woman say, 'Little calf in pasture
could turn out a bull-mother.'

Man-dread say, 'when money done
woman love done!'
Woman say 'Just like a good rum
woman go with a good man.'

Man-dread say, 'Marriage got teeth!'
Woman say, 'Marriage is *sweet sweet*,'

So, man and woman come
hold hands and say,
'The two of we so full of love
the two of we jus *have* to love.'

Haiku Moments: 3

9

Your spinning days worked
generations without pay –
O windmill here, dead!

10

Falling leaf scares him
yet out he strolls under trees –
does autumn test him?

11

With all of the storm –
thunder, winds, floods – whole rock sits
there loving the ground,

12

Forgetting the pains
of childbirth again she's there
and now the birth-yell!

13

Water cut, lights fail,
now making little love, look
she gone dead asleep.

14

Miss Kate's water pan
hot on head: in hand is fan
and hymnbook to church.

15

Nine-Night singing sad,
merry, nonstop – an owl hoots
in the one silence.

16

Thief thief mi one-goat,
hog-sick kill mi sow, Jesas,
now mi plantain cut!

17

Sun-hot sun-hot why
you wahn black-man sweat so like
him drink river up?

18

Her hands like a child's
work her flute sonata voice
and pull out my tooth.

Meeting Mr Cargill on My Village Road

Down from his donkey letting it
freely crop roadside weeds,
he shakes my hand grandly warm.
'Bless mi eye them now,' he says,
'Cousin Olmassa son, yu home.
Home from Englan! And fine fine
yu look. Like Christmas come
home-boy, whey yu stan up!

'And now, the world have
no father fo you.
Come home to find we bury him,
yu Olmassa, under yu mango tree.'

'I shave yu sleepin ol man.
I help bathe him,
give him he *last last* wash.
We dress him,
put him in he blacksuit and tie.
We lay him out, lay him out
in he own cedar board box, shinin.'

'Graveside bring everybody,
in full heart, full voice,
a-let him go in prayers and hymns,
a-give him he sixfoot down
and show a deserving traveller gone
to rest all him eighty-odd year.'

'And Nine-Night pass, at yu house.
Home yu didn come. But all,
everything, everything, happen
like yu was here, here on spot.'

Next time in my home village,
I didn't see Mr Cargill.
I saw only the new mound of earth
his own coffin replaced.

Starapple Time Starapple Trees

All around flame-trees blaze
a red acreage of domed tops.
Mouths are sweet stained.

Everybody eats the starapple.
Brown or purple or white
succulent ready flesh exposes
hidden star to open faces
of starapple time,

Enticing to be opened in
group-loving starapple time,
lips-luring round fruits grew
between limbs, growing
shadowed to readiness
near big boat cotton-tree erect,
washed by burning sun.

And apple-honey squeezed and sucked –
all else gone suspended –
who won't make joy noises
under canopy of coppery silk,
bridal in sunlight? Even
a woodpecker, in its dipping
flight, screams with laughter.

A Walk Through Kingston, Jamaica

My peripheral eye caught
familiar angles. I knew he hid
with the waiting people
of the city's backland.

My steps halted,
in joy in fear,
beside a bowed wreck.

It was a busily suspicious face,
something seldom aroused,
the clothes a stink nest.
My memory sharpened the jolly
stutterer at school.

My anxious voice bounced loose
like an old embrace of boyhood.
Leo, man! I said.

A glare unlidded his old
froggy eyes. A rush of memory opened
his mouth and arms. A twist
hardened a contemptuous mouth
in a knotted beard.

He slowly drew a final door.
It seemed my voice,
my dress, my look, wounded him
as if I was a foreign reporter,
to expose him, to say
he chickened out on his children.

His word staggering manhood
had linked his first girl, I knew.
He had sustained a fluency
of eight new lives. I knew
he had left them, years now.

But I knew him before all that.
Leo! My voice pulled
at his hurried and ragged turn away.
My early village friend was armless
and wordless for me.

Was this the final man?
There was no joke,
no touch.

Leo! I whispered.
His shuffles mounted
a wider and wider distance.

Defendant in a Jamaican Court

Yes I did chop him, sar.
I chop him.
I woz full-full
of the vexation of spirit, sar.

I woz beyon all ow I know me, sar –
over the odda side cut off
from all mi goodness
and I couldn steady mi han firm, sar.

I chop him shoulder.
I let mi distric man blood stream down.

Him did storm up mi bad-bad waters
that I couldn settle –
that flood me, sar –
that mek one quick-quick terrible shut-eye
when all mi badness did rule.

Words of a Jamaican Laas Moment Them

When I dead
mek rain fall.
Mek the air wash.
Mek the lan wash good-good.
Mek dry course them run, and run.

As laas breath gone
mek rain burst –
hilltop them work
waterfall, and all
the gully them gargle fresh.

Mek breadfruit limb them drip,
mango limb them drip. Cow, hog, fowl
stan still, in the burst of clouds.
Poinciana bloom them soak off, clean-clean.
Grass go unda water.

Instant I gone
mek all the Island wash – wash away
the mess of my shortcomings –
all the brok-up things I did start.
Mi doings did fall short too much.
Mi ways did hurt mi wife too oftn.

Worse Than Poor

Lord poor man poor
    him worse than poor
him is real miser
    and none the wiser

Him av one coin
    him wash the coin
and to av some silver
    him drink the water

126

Villager's Independence: 1

Every meal-time going be a meal-time.
Every child body going have clothes.
Every child going go school everyday.
Instead of a hurricane mash-up
it going be a hurricane of build-up.
And every house stan up to breeze-blow.

We going have a tractor to farm we land.
Woman head burden of load going to go
all along on four-wheel.
Rain-season rain not going sink. A new
reservoir going keep rainfall fo dry-time.
We going build up a real market.

Foot-track them going broaden out
into crossroad after crossroad them.
Big Pasture will turn new house settlement.
Aeroplane going come land in Bottom Wood
clearance. Ship across the world going stop
right here outside we Long Bay Beach.

Water like power going come live in
we house – a suitable quiet partner
always there with lectric light.
And when Queen-of-Englan come,
we going house her and home her
right here in we district.

Drum soun come and come through Island now
drummin hell spirit out everybody
and everything. Not to turn back.
It here. Not ever to go away.
Me hearing it good-good. All the new
new soun of mento full up me head.

Before God and before man
a change a-come.
It a-come.
Overdue, overdue, in we life!
Before God and before man
Independence a-come!

Villager's Independence: 2

Me not a poor man. Not a poor man.
Me dohn beg. Not lazy. Not sick.
Me have good houseful a children.
It only that mi boots in pieces
and me get swamp-over,
turn in a wretch *bad bad*,
with piece a rundown land
with dry-time, no donkey, no milking cow.

But, me not a poor man. Not a poor man.
Me a healthy man in charge
a mi little house, mi family, mi taxes.
It only that mi shirt is patchwork
on patch on mi back
and me get swamp-over,
turn in a wretch *bad bad*,
in a wet house with roof not get repair
and too much night-time bellyache groaning.

But, me not a poor man. Not a poor man.
Me a fit man. Rich in heart
and body and mind. Full a desire.
It only that mi mouth mash up.
Teeth them drop out and gone.
And me get swamp-over,
turn in a wretch *bad bad*,
with too much bony people them
touching me and crowding me
with bad-talk wrong-word them
what come back and come back and settle
every night in we house.

But when Jesus did say: the poor
you have with you always,
him didn mean me at all!
Me not a Poor man! Never was.
And Independence a-come to prove that!

Woman at Waterhole

>   Lord
> we waterhole –
> we well –
> we waterhole dry.
> It dry up.

>   Breeze-blow flattn we house
>   and mud-up we things
>   like before
>   and before.
>   Flood kill off we crop them
>   and make the children moan
>   like before
>   and before.

> Now waterhole dry
> We well –
> we waterhole dry up.

>   Who goin stop sky-fire
>   roast-up of we?
>   Who go save we one-cow
>   and one-pig and one-goat?
>   Who goin save the children them, O?

>   Lord
> waterhole dry up.
> We well –
> we waterhole dry.
> O – it dry up.

Masked People, One People

Is we in a tinkle-jangle of bells and beads –
we – who play more than man-and-woman breed
in artworks
at footworks
in limbs a-rage
in rhythm rampage.
    Is everybody the carnival.

We group up CRESCENT-AND-STAR.
We group up PATCHWORK PAUPERS.
Is you and me GREAT QUEENS AND KINGS.
Is we turn GOLDEN WINGED-THINGS.
We group up LEO
and group up VIRGO.
We group up POCO PEOPLE
and BALMYARD PEOPLE.
    Is everybody the carnival.

Is you and me with chants
dispelling wants.
Is we like caged birds flown
in sharp whistles blown,
wild in sunshine on and on
in drums and beat of pan
with spears pointed up
and flags that flap.
    Is everybody the carnival.

We group up MASAI WARRIORS
and ABORIGINE RAIN DANCERS.
We group up DEVILS AND PRIESTS
and BUDDHA'S FOOTPRINTS.
We group up FERTILTY GODDESSES
and RELEVANCE OF SNAKES.
Look how he's ALL HAIR OUT OF A CAVE
and she TWO LOCKED HEARTS OF LOVE.
    Is everybody the carnival.

Look how she is BAD BABYLON WITH GUNS
and he DRAGON
and he CHIEF OF AMERICAN INDIAN
stuck in a dance delirium.
Is we the silver trees of COURTING MACAWS,
HUMMINGBIRDS AND JACKDAWS.
Listen at back at the cry
for SUPERNATURAL WORLD going by.
    Is everybody the carnival.

Is you and me group up TRAILING CAPES.
We group up STILTS AND SHADOW SHAPES.
Is we treble NINE MUSES
and group up BEST OF WITCHES.
Is you and me group up OGUN PEOPLE
and KRISHNA PEOPLE.
Look how she is ALL OF LEGBA
and he OUTRAGEOUS ROBBER.
    Is everybody the carnival.

Is you and me in a different glamour
raving with foreigner
like ANGEL OF PEACE
and she MEPHISTOPHELES
like he, a dull worker, is SOWER
and she, entrancing death, is REAPER.
Is you and me out of worlds
into worlds.
    Is everybody the carnival.

We group up a PHARAOH.
We group up SHANGO.
Look how whole of world, he's ATLAS
and she, falcon-faced, is HORUS.
Look at SWEETBOY FLIRT
and she, dripping jewels, is ALL OF WOMAN'S MIRTH.
Is you and me in a bacchanal
in a burru crowd jump-up for all.
    Is everybody the carnival.

Is we in loud horns and shouts
for GROUPS OF HARLOTS
with HERCULES AND HEBE
and ARISTOCRATIC ANANCY –
straight and round and round
through the town spellbound
in street
of music beat.
    Is everybody the carnival.

Is you and me,
is we,
in sounds of RUM PEOPLE
and SUN PEOPLE,
in sounds of SUNFIRE
and sounds of SUKUYA,
in a trance of the dance,
we who'll never cut the raging pulse.

    Is everybody the carnival,
    everybody the carnival,
    steel music, drumbeat.
    Is we in the heat
    revelling, having a shout,
    in a break from day-in-day-out...

Everyday Traveller

Taximan sees me today.
Sees me waving him down.
Again switches off
his FOR HIRE light.
Speeds up, passes me.

Similar. So similar
to our train driver
when he was late.
We passengers echoed
happy relief to see him.

Singled me out, at a glance.
Exploded in my face:
'You black bastard!
you keep your shit shut!'

On and on, on and on,
my ordinary face
confronts this
helpless defining
translated 'vulnerable'.

Millennium Eyes

We could never see enough.
We gleaned only a little of what is.
A hidden past little understood
a future view still out of sight
we could never engage with a full account.

Nothing outside was believable
as the image seen. Delivered words
carried omissions and additions
and stayed with closed faces
when seeing exactly was crucial.

And we yearned. We yearned to see
to the bottom of reasons,
through walls and over horizons.
We needed others to absorb that violence
in the seared flesh of our pain
and see our needs
and their rooted establishments –
see all of a situation,
all of an outcome
with all its angles, way back to source.

Now astrology tells us
the millennium brings new eyes:
make eyes, wear them openly, you grow
more and more eyes inwardly.
And colleges start up eyemaking courses –
a craze with students everywhere now.

In shades of grey, green and diamond,
brown, orange, blue, black and purple,
worn as pendants or bracelets
or as a band around the head,
eyes are the latest adornments.

Couples newly wed stare into
each other's manufactured eyes:
people say they see their future in them.
And crowned, bangled, garlanded, hung
with eyes, student groups go about singing
'More eyes, more eyes, more eyes!
The millennium brings new eyes!'

Words at My Mother's Funeral
(Maud Berry: 21.2.1897 – 10.7.1990)

While poinciana trees bloomed for sunlight
and mullets moved in the rivers,
unnoticed, quiet quiet you left,
completing footsteps and heartbeats
where ninety-three years halted.
And now, to your stay that marked us
we mark your going.
   O, mother, go well.

While sea waves rolled out on Fair Prospect beach
you vacated the house
in a silence at noon
ending a vessel that gave
one woman and five men
who in turn gave
their own little crowd you also mothered.
And we grew in your mothercraft:
your foodmaking, your sewing,
your artworks of hands and voices,
your touches now channelled under my skin,
your many pieces of songs in my head.
And I remember, you knew
when my tummy needed a rub
with the sign of the cross on it
and knew too when my tummy didn't really ache.
Like a season, you came to an end.
   O, mother, go well.

While a mongoose looked both ways to cross a track
you made your exit, but stay scattered
in memory, well highlighted, instinctive
and determined, to subdue and manage
each day's delivery of old losses not reckoned
in fresh nakedness, starvation, yelling
and accidents. Yet, with all the strength
of a horse in your mother-knowing
your sight became darkness
and your memory became confusion.

But hadn't you given yourself a patient daughter
to closely share your challenges and body pains?
Like a tree unfolding the sun's work
wasn't your giving your achievements
and your suffering an encounter you withstood?
    O, mother, go well.

While banana leaves and coconut limbs pointed
up towards the wide brightness
you left, where, so hard to win,
a strong heart prolonged you to endure
a new struggle of no-release
through months, weeks, days
when standing or sitting
like your lying down through all
the daylight and darkness was all agony.
Was this your purifying fire
that in waiting in the years before
had made you sing, over and over:
I will not let thee go Dear Lord;
I will not let thee go.
I will wrestle with thee till the break of day;
I will not let thee go?
    O, mother, go well.

While a woodpecker flew in a dipping flight
you made your departure.
Often, in these last years of pain
you remembered your husband
who'd gone before you thirtythree years.
But, always, your talk stayed
on your parents and your childhood home,
a place your yearning was fixed on.
And from the darkness, a streak of light emerged.
    O, mother, go full and free in love.
        O, mother, go well.

People with Maps

Unused, talents withered early
or were withering
going malformed in city slums,
in villages around shacks in drought,
in hunger, in loss of hope.

Street wandering, I walked into marchers
shouting 'Hurrah!' and blowing horns, beating
drums, and playing violins with announcements:
'Pains of nations united. All-nations'
abundance work declared!'

Impatient and confused, I rushed about asking
for more news. I am told, 'Visionaries are here
on the bridge, in sessions, with own teams.'

'Who are they?' I asked. 'Who are they?'
'Some heads of seminars are Tagore
and Matisse, Tolstoy and Mary Seacole,
Martin L. King, de Beauvoir, Fanon,
Leadbelly, Mozart, Montessori, Einstein.'

I ran to the end of the bridge where it opened
on to many roads. The heads of seminars had left.
Breathless I saw the new teams of people with maps.
They made notes of the many-pronged roadsigns:
to 'The University of World's Connection' villages.

Reply from Mother Africa

To your letter of outburst, your outcry
of spirit long overdue,
I will now reply.

Consider diverse difference. How movement
generates the many parts of life,
to release their own union.
And how trust is enshrined in oneness
undeniably. And your move
would observe trust. And time
for your ancestors' change had come.
            Consider.

Consider how a supplier –
like mountains of compost
like waterhole or loaded ship
or a calabash of fufu or wine,
serving birth, serving that
lonely loser, the bull elephant
consumed at the edge of the forest,
serving bleached grass brittly crackling
where dust sheets leap in dance
and, after August grazing pounded the grass,
November rains to water new growing –
how I facilitate.

I remember –
I watch migrating birds take off
and watch birds arrive.
I watch storks pick up lizards running away
from bursting fires under savanna sky,
watch a meercat stand erect on lookout duty,
other eyes watchful for movements
as finger-lipping rhinos pick leaves
and other square mouths firmly crop grass.
I watch zebras run with two-toed ostriches.
A lion hugging a zebra, kiss-capping its mouth
and nose. Monkeys find seeds, flowers,
fruits, birds and a baby gazelle.

I watch hunting dogs disgorge meat for puppies.
Watch a kissing bug suck a caterpillar dry
and a bird take the bug.
Round and round the zero hour,
I provide the means for meetings for movement,
not the movement itself.
            Consider. Consider.

Consider how
the lion defines the zebra
as a meal to devour. Yet
wallowing in it and absorbing it
signals a compelling love,
a companionship in the flesh,
not a self-inspired love
but a driven and a violating love.

I remember –
a denial is a dispossessing,
a dispossessing is a devouring.

I remember –
a tribal will suggests
a possession of the whole world
alone, with only its own lookalikes.

I remember –
to be fixed within boundaries
for denial, you were renamed 'Negro'
and classified 'nonwhite', 'minority',
'underclass', 'ethnic', 'Third World'.
                    Consider your place, fully.

Consider –
in a dry season ever present
available pools and streams absent.
Faces released easily in symbolic light
add bars around faces in symbolic night.
An all-people network?
Hidden summers, hidden voices, in zero?
An all-human spirit inhabiting change?

I remember –
driven by dread
and violations and hidden compulsions
and lookalike self preferences,
like packs, like vultures, like prides –
round and round with the rotating sun –
movement is endless.

Reunion

Five hundred years
before reunion –
Mother Africa.

And here I am.
Here I am, where
at the beginning
one sun brushed me
in silence
and I became
obsessed lover of dance.

Here are these eyes,
these eyes around me –
unfathomable.

I do not know.
I do not know
one house
of my ancestral line.

I cannot grasp.
I cannot grasp
one word
in the voices I hear.

And yet
time has kept
every face my own –
every face my own, looking
like a house of exorcism, well lit.

Approach me.
Approach me
drums, whistles, chants.

I hear the time
of day one.

Reinitiate,
rededicate,
O all of me.

Reconsecrate my place
in every day:
valid like earth
with water
with sun
with air,
with one and every season.

I see
each different face,
like mine –
its own part
a symbol in a time
with its charge.

And, in me, at first:
I am a tree
never to be cut;
second: I am a word
reserved for ceremony;
third: I am a presence
never violated.

I am end.
I am beginning.
I am co-sharer.
I am a piece of the whole.
I am participator.
I am participator.

We dance.
We dance in dust.
We dance. We dance. We dance.

With found faces and drumming,
with found faces and drumming,
I am new spirit out of skin.
I am new spirit out of skin,
with found faces and drumming...

Going About

I go in the belly of the running stream
and go in the feet of wind whisking by

I fly from where the road ended
and stay in footsteps gone

I go with the death dot of a flame
and stay with the last moment of the year

I go with sea wave into sand
and stay with day's merging with night

I search I search I search
where all times missed accumulate

Windrush Songs

(2007)

Wind-rush

I'd like to set out a storm
watching it like the dream it is
watching the sea come
emptying its folds of boats

Watching towering palmtrees fall
across the backs of running cattle
watching the wind carry trees
and drop them on top of shack roofs

Hearing leaves of branches whistle –
I won't miss how breezeblow madness
batter and beat the place up island-wide
knocking things over with sea raging and raging

How island-wide bugle-blow of wind
batter and mash-up the place

break up big limb and banana leaf-them
in nothing but a day of wind-rush –
screaming
            plundering
                        crying.

Wash of Sunlight

Oh, the sun has washed me,
penetrated my skin, my body,
my ways of open fields, and imprinted me
with the glow of sunrise and sunset.

I marvel at the burst of seeds to sunlight
and the careless giving of water over rocks.

Watching the sun rising
I feel I have more than its force in me.
Like the sun overhead at midday
I feel much greater distances
are here sunken in me.

Watching the moon reflected in water,
held by the awe of water,
held by awesome feelings, I know
much greater and more awesome depths
somewhere inside of me.

I stand on the land. I touch
fire, touch water, feel air.

Sitting up Past Midnight

I used to get up some midnight
and come sit at mi doorway
a-think, a-think, a-smoke mi pipe.

I a-think about mi crops –
about mi fields of yams and bananas,
worryin about breeze-blow-hurricane
breakin up mi yam vines an blowin down
mi full banana bunches, ready fo market.

I a-think about mi donkey
how him is sick and don't get up.
Him just picky picky –
a straw stay in his mouth
and him don't chew it.

I a-think about mi third boy child –
always learnin lessons in lamplight –
readin bright-bright, recitin bible passage-them,
now him need extra teachin for examination
and how, how I gwan pay extra teachin?

Then I get strange feelin, a-think
back on mi ancestors them and slave life.
I realise how much of mi history I can't fill in.

Yet – I wake up to come sit
at mi doorway, thinkin,
thinkin about that dead past of mine

seein how mi life face midnight
widhout one lamplight.

Desertion

Dicko Parks gone from him house
and wife, children, dog, donkey
and the land-piece him jus start planting.

Dicko Parks lef not one clue
to show if him gone up, down
or if him vanish sideways
like when him lef Africa
inside him forefathers them.

Him taxes not paid.
Water come down through him roof.
Him stray donkey taken into pound
cos it ol rope bust up.

Three long months now come and gone.
Dicko Parks lef like him gone to him land –
no nightfall bring him back since.
Him wet-eye wife stop search and inquire.
Him sad sad children still skip and play.

I African They Say

I hear people say I African, yet
I know I never seen one, never hear one
and dohn know who he is at all.

If I talk African, is
no more than water a-babble
or bird a-sing at day-clean.

I hear some people say
I dance like African. Yet, fo me, I do
no more than breeze a ruffle tree top.

Africa a blank in mi head
like slave plantations – gone.
I was always at sea, lost.

My ancestors, unknown or despised,
like strangers who threaten me –
I was always lost, at sea.

Harnessed, overworked, never paid,
like any horse or mule,
ancestors were all at sea.

Africa threw ancestors to wild raging sea –
Africa never gestured care to restore me –
just as Africa sold and abandoned me
I can never consider Africa.

Old Slave Villages

The windmills are dead
Their tombs are empty towers

Where high estate walls are broken down
wire fences control the boundaries

Thatched slave shacks are gone
In their place – zinc houses, gardens

The great houses, now derelict,
turned to school grounds – or hotels

The vast fields of sugar cane
are pastures, with cattle grazing

The tombs of landscape windmills
are broken empty towers.

Poverty Life

Hungry children keep hungry mothers
hungry mothers rear hungry children
and children go to school on nothing.

With land, two mules and a bicycle
a man can dance and get drunk
in the mouldy, sweet musky smell of dirty lives –
held captive by poverty.

Like captive by slavery
captive by poverty is
a continuous memory.

Leave the country for the town
to sit in bare earth backyards
or walk the streets hustling
threatened by rentman, police and rats.

Wear lucky garbage shoes
clothes wash and patch
pick up bottles to sell for bread.
Go home to broken windows
rainstained ceilings and walls.

Not enough of anything except children.
Working children are truanting children
or hustling children
or children listless
in the sticky heat of muddy earth floor.

Poverty Ketch Yu an Hol Yu

A trap ketch yu, naked
an hol yu dere, naked!

Yu ketch up ina poverty trap
Great House get yu fi servant
Great House dog keep yu it servant

Cokanut oil will shine up yu hair
you trousers press sharp sharp –
but pocket dem empty, empty like husk

Then man you throw you trousers –
only throw you trousers on the bed –
few days later, man, she pregnant again!

A morning time take yu
an swing yu like dead puss
then – it pick yu up again
an swing yu like dead puss

Seven day a week man
seven day a week
you a-move like dead puss.

Sea-Song One

Come on
Seawash of travel
Expose new layers of skin

Come on calm voice of sea
Come and settle on land

Sea's tumble wash
Change our rags for riches

Come on – tumble wash of sea
Clear away the bloody waters
      Clear away the bloody waters

Reasons for Leaving Jamaica

Mi one milkin' cow did jus' die!
Gone, gone – an' leave me worthless
like hurricane disaster.

Then, mi neighbour stoned, stoned
and killed mi dog, and I did know
I would move – move well away.

Man, when I did come happy, happy to reap
mi first four bunch of bananas
from mi new half acre of land
and, man, find every one newly cut and gone –
I did move about shattered,
dazed in a crazy spin of a dream.

That half acre did take me ten year to buy –
mi little land-piece of bananas was
mi pride an' hope an' sense of achievement.
Now, a man did come and reap mi first crop.
I did know there and then that if I did kill him,
him couldn't come back and come back!

Then, man, I did go tired, tired.
Like miself, mi piece of land
did sit there tired – tired.
Windrush did jus'come an' save me an' him.

To Travel This Ship

To travel this ship, man
I gladly strip mi name
of a one-cow, two-goat an a boar pig
an sell the land piece mi father lef
to be on this ship and to be a debtor.

Man, jus fa diffrun days
I woulda sell, borrow or thief
jus fa diffrun sunrise an sundown
in annodda place wid odda ways.

To travel this ship, man
I woulda hurt, I woulda cheat or lie,
I strip mi yard, mi friend and cousin-them
to get this yah ship ride.

Man – I woulda sell mi modda
jus hopin to buy her back.
Down in dat hole I was
I see this lickle luck, man,
I see this lickle light.

Man, Jamaica is a place
where generations them start out
havin notn, earnin notn,
and – dead – leavin notn.

I did wake up every mornin
and find notn change.
Children them shame to go to school barefoot.
Only a penny to buy lunch.

Man, I follow this lickle light for change.
I a-follow it, man!

A Dream of Leavin

Man, so used to notn, this is
a dream I couldn't dream of dreamin,
so – I scare I might wake up.

One day I would be Englan bound!
A travel would have me on sea
not chained down below, every tick of clock,
but free, man! Free like tourist!

Never see *me* coulda touch world of Englan –
when from all accounts I hear
that is where all we prosperity end up.

I was always in a dream of leavin.
My half-finished house was on land
where work-laden ancestors' bones lay.

The old plantation land still stretch-out
    down to the sea,
        giving grazing to cattle.

Work Control Me Fadda Like a Mule

Work control me fadda like a mule,
control me modda like a jackass,
yet, stubborn stubborn,
life pass we
an *that* we full house live on.

Circle of hard time suck out we place
hold we like bad obeah spell
have we like skeletons –
starvation beget we.

Hungriness develop me
like rock a-want wings-them
but sunshine flood me,
and roast me and dry me inside.

152

But, rain bring hope
and wet me tongue and toes-them.
Rain-storm drench me
and sea-water wash me.

And now, sea a-carry me
headlong to a little change –
and here me a-shake
with hopefulness
      about what I goin *do* with it.

Reminiscence Voice

Man, I want to go back to hear
hilltop cockcrow giving
answer to bottom yard rooster challenge
mother cow giving anxious 'moo'
for a calf keeping cool in the shade –
      I want to renew all that.

Man, I want to go back to hear
cooing of ground-doves in quiet noon-time
and tree-top nightingales singing
to the moon long before daylight –
      I want to renew all that.

Man, I want to go back to have
a curry-goat feed under coconut palms
rum flowing like a nature stream
and conchshell blowing for a big sea catch –
      I want to renew all that.

Man, I want to go back to hear
Maama Tunny passing to church
fanning herself, calling
      'Good-morning' to our house.

The Rock

Me not goin back to dat hell Jamaica.
Me have more pain there than I can tell.
Sun-hot burn me up outside –
rain wahn drown me inside mi house.

Me dohn go back to no damn Jamaica
wha all-a-we call – 'The Rock'.
Rocky road burst up me toe-dem.
Hungry belly wahn me walk like skeleton.

Me not gohn back Jamaica.
Only white-man-dem –
users of mi mind an body –
call Jamaica paradise:
not me, made from sweat an curse.

I leavin the Rock.
I dohn intend to go back.
Only outside people-dem call Jamaica 'beautiful'.

So-so breadfruit not gohn force me to eat it.
Dry time not gohn have me shrivel-up.
Satday night not gohn find me an empty pocket
listenin foolishness in-a rum-bar.

No sar – early cockcrow fa wake-up
not gohn drag me outa bed to starve me.
Monday to Monday gohn find me – absent!
Mi jackass no-pay force me to move.

Me not gohn back Jamaica.
Only poverty there mould a man.
Only touris-dem see it paradise.
No sar! That sea sound not gohn reach me.
Ground dove cooin not gohn fill-up mi ears.

Thinkin of Joysie

When I think of Joysie, man,
I goin wahn fly back instantly –
but, Joysie dohn like hurry-hurry
even though she the rudest village girl.

Joysie is a winna, all sweeta,
she give you what she have
like she is belly of the movin sea
but, calm, she jus like an early dusk
afta sleep satisfy you good, good.

Joysie can cry out like you kill her
when you hear her cry out, saying:
You, you, you think you is Jesus
opening Paradise door!
And so wiry, you cahn believe how she move.

Joysie has the bigges heart,
the stronges body, most cutting scream.
She takes you like a tidal wave
takes a canoe, leavin sea, sky
an jus one little bird.

Man, Joysie have hot temper
but her big big givin is cool.
Joysie make sure you cahn forget her.
Joysie has no keep-quiet manners –
half the village men *love* Joysie.

Fish Talk

Talk about mi oily-mout dish –
then talk only fish.

Fried fish, stewed fish, creole and escovitch fish
or jus red snapper in papillote

Man – notn make me forget
great crab-back flake

Or creamed lobster with butter and
stamp-and-go saltfish frittas

Give me plateful of little sprats fried up
an spiced with pepper, salt, pimento grains

Man I sweat – gone in the mood
jus talkin nice peppery food.

Sun-Hot Drink

1

Jelly-coconut water –
from baby coconut growing –
full of water inside.
Drunk in the field, man, in sun-hot:
break coconut's thick husk with machete
and, sweating, open it –
find the inside white river
find coolness, man, fruitiness,
that soft sweet taste
from sun, tree, air.

2

Sunlight's dominion claims
water, water, man, water:
you get one drink
and you're gone, man
down stream
like a log afloat wallowing off
all sweat. And you move
again. Move again, man.

3

White rum, white rum: man
that's fabric of sun caught
to be reborn inside of you
and have you laced from head
to toe, burning, man, sweet, sweet!

Empire Day

Empire Day is what me rememba, singin
praises to Modder Country, Englan.
At home, me put on mi church shoes
an mi new likkle khaki trousers an shirt
an meet other spruced-up distric
children-them. Stiffly, happily on we go.

At school, we have prayers. We recite
poems about Englan and Empire. Each
one of us get a likkle Union Jack
and sweets with flags printed
all over the tin.

Other schools join we. And, drilled,
marchin around the schoolyard, aroun
our wide and high, high poinciana tree
covered wid red flowers, our likkle
Union Jack them a-wave and a-flutta.

We sing we heart out, singing 'Rule
Britannia', glowin with all we loyal
virtue to King, Country and Empire.

In jollification, we play games.
We eat jerk pork, fresh bread, candy
an spicy cake. We eat snowball an drink
cool drinks. Mi Union Jack sweets-tin
turn mi treasure, keeping
mi slate pencil an mi marble-them.

Old Slave Plantation Village Owner

She lived alone with many dogs:
the rich white queen of our village.
My father and my brother worked for her.
I worked as her teenage butler and
nursed her pet bulldog, that she worshipped.

Nearly all the village ancestors
had laboured for her ancestors
as house slaves, field slaves,
sugar plantation slaves:
she was respected as a royal person.

Her modern fenced-off house with broad verandahs,
built on foundations of the Old Great House,
was near the ruins of the sugar mill
on raised ground, with gardens.
Her lands were like an ocean around her.

She inherited no culture, nor developed any,
of assisting slave descendants
with education, health, or advancement.
She entertained the rich
in celebrations, under electric stars.
Everything in her house was shining.

She would not assist my further education –
yet she would sit me down
in a cushioned fall-back chair
and play her piano to me,
using me as audience.

And first European music
to impress me deeply, played
on His Master's Voice gramophone,
was her favourite record and love song:
John McCormack's tenor voice
singing 'Yours is my heart alone'.

A boy cannot caress
a grand lady's isolated heart:
he is less than her dogs.
He takes her outrages and curses
on serving her food and cleaning her rum glasses,
her shoes, her ashtrays.
In moonlight, between shaven hedges
of jasmine, among whitewashed palm tree trunks,
he serves answers to questions
about village gossip.

I heard the nightingale
and never mentioned it.
You were a crystal voice, perfumed.
I gave you honour for your wealth –
    created by whip and gun.

Comparing Now with Ancestors' Travel from Africa

The first time when ancesta-them did travel
them did a-travel to lose tongue, name
and pay. This time, descendant-them
a-travel by choice, with hope, and with
resolution for fulfilment.

The first time when ancesta-them did travel
them did a-travel pile up in a ship hole,
chained-up, angry, filthy, half starved.
This time descendant-them a-travel free
a-si moonlight on big sea.

The first time when ancesta-them did travel
them did a-travel to reach shore bruise up, half dead.
Some leave them bones a-push about by big sea.
This time, descendant-them a-travel
to reach in-a clean Sunday clothes.

The first time when ancesta-them did travel
them did a-travel in-a dread bout
where they would reach, and specially
would they reach as meat on white-man table.

This time, descendant-them, head full of hope,
droppin off all the past – a-look forward
to a-share skills, wealth and recognition –
determined to be humanly respected.

And some may yet a-travel
to write down them ancesta story.

A Story I Am In

They thought we were lost, wandering
more than they were.
Their leader pulled his gun and wounded
one of us, we tried to help our wounded.
They tied us to walk with their wagons.

We became lost in time.
The days buzzed their arrivals
and their worn paths of departures:
no saviour in the world.

And like trees' absorption of sun change
at work, our flame sometimes ignited
bright flashes, while mostly
smouldering, fading, dying little by little.

We were drilled to know that
our tongues moved like leaden frogs,
our hands were blunt machetes,
our milkers reported we gave dirt
and ashes.

And waiting on slow time
we sang sadly in chains
not seeing the gold our hands wove.

They staged us showing how well
we splintered stones with our hands,
carried a mule on our backs,
ate rags, wood shavings and shit

They talked like clanging metal,
fought like bulls clashing heads,
using voices like sea sounds in caves.

Devoured, our time was their sweetness of meat
and their energy of power.
Every day sunrises herded us
into fields that ground us like mills.

And our blood premium – Sugar –
hoisted the flags of kings
and made their horns of power music.

Mi Fight with Jack-Jack

I wonda, always wonda, if
mi fight with Jack-Jack didn kill him.

Satday evening, everybody at village square –
Jack-Jack an me there – fo death.

Since we fight, Jack-Jack never is
that man him was like before.

Since we fight, him head droop
an him nevva walk straight again.

Jack-Jack walk with a hold-up
Like sometn did cut – up in him hip.

Jack-Jack did hit me to kill me.
Him give me pain I neva, neva did feel.

Jack-Jack did pick me up, lick me down
and jump up-and-down in-a mi face.

Him did fight me to kill me dead –
I did fight him with *all* mi vengeance.

Mi head, mi hand, mi heart, all
did hit him, hurt him, overpower him.

If Jack-Jack did have him machete
him woulda chop me up –

him woulda lash me up all over
with straight straight streak of blood.

Him did fight me to kill me dead –
I did fight him to stay on mi foot.

I believe – I know – we fight did kill him.
Him did suffer fram it bad.

162

We fight did slow-slow make him sink
and in time go rotten-rotten.

When I go to Englan now
I goin sen him wife some money,

I goin sen Jack-Jack wife money.
I goin sen him wife some money – regular.

How the Weak Manufactured Power for the Strong

Days washed my generations
like showers of rain that sunk,
vanished in drought,
and we were like rocks.

Rooted in stones and flaming sunlight
the weak worked, and made power for the strong.

Now I go to live with people I helped –
with users of painful power.

I go to live with the unfeeling eaters
who digested the proceeds of my ancestors.
I go driven to fulfil sharing.

I go with bright smiles and awkward speech,
the tree feller, land digger, planter –
the non-harvester.

Awakener of new knowing in the knower
I go to live with faces of elegance and pride –

I who look as if
rooted in stones in sunlight.

Englan Voice

I prepare – an prepare well – fe Englan.
Me decide, and done leave behine
all the voice of ol slave-estate bushman.

None of that distric bad-talk in Englan,
that bush talk of ol slave-estate man.

Hear me speak in Englan, an see
you dohn think I a Englan native.

Me nah go say
'Bwoy, how you du?'
me a-go say 'How are you old man?'

Me nah go say
'Wha yu nyam las night?'
me a-go say 'What did you have for supper?'

Patois talk is bushman talk –
people who talk patois them dam lazy.

Because mi bush voice so settle in me
an might let me down in-a Englan
me a-practise.

Me a-practise talk like teacher
till mi Englan voice come out-a me
like water from hillside rock.

Even if you fellows here
dohn hear mi Englan voice
I have it – an hear it in mi head!

A Greater Oneness

Man, I goin Englan to speed up
what Empire start – that scorn, self-love and pride, I will
put together with humility.

I believe daylight and night-time are partners.
Night covers the day with arms like wings
to leave earth to gestate.

Man, I believe daylight and night-time married
and do proliferate Nature's children –

Man, I see it that all faces of difference
will come together with one face –

walking with multifarious faces,
with love, with peace, with essential growing.

Man, from where this world has come
we cannot be chance-experiment.
We are willing learners and givers
from provisions given.

Man, cruelty is our early wildness
to be more and more tamed
into the untarnished glow of lovingness.

Man – I goin to Englan
to help speed up Englan
into a greater oneness
with an ever growing humanity.

New Space

I lived where the day's light was
a clean and open transparency
so clear I should see into level distances
and, from hilltops,
know every fluttering wing,
every leaf down to the sprawling sea.

I should know every sky glow
and be dreaming in
the white sheeting of moonlight –
moonlight's wide sheeting.

I should be well washed
by clean green spaces and the gargle
of clear and stony streams, invisible
on sheer bird-throated land.

I should sway and echo with
the ancient sea's voice
and its depths, pregnant with life
more varied than the air holds –

longing to stand on the feet of a passing day
        and be carried
                where all new time is stored.

In the Land and Sea Culture-crossed

In the land and sea culture-crossed
we call to the hearts of difference.
Restless, we widen our boundaries.
Expansion may be for self-loving, yet
our world is smaller and closer
and, in gesturing, we touch different other.

A voice in me says:
Completeness comes from
a balance of allness.
All faces and conditions you not
only inherit but with them must find
agreement and oneness.

A voice in me says: Who is not
a beginner, seeking balance?
Who does not want to be heights and depths of music
harmonious with all difference?

A voice in me says:
We will change wildness to love,
into rejuvenation.
There is madness in self-love
we will change it to sanity.
We will release change in each other.

As the ground catches the rotten fruit
for its centre to grow again, and
as only our *negative* selves are hurt by cleansing
for the expansion of self essence,
oh, let us more and more know.

Let us strive for
a coming together of allness in the self,
as, at peace with our centre
inhabiting all faces
inhabiting the core of all centres
being at home with allness
we strive to become habitation of allness.

Beginning in a City, 1948

Stirred by restlessness, pushed by history,
I found myself in the centre of Empire.
Those first few hours, with those packed impressions
I never looked at in all these years.

I knew no room. I knew no Londoner.
I searched without knowing.
I dropped off my grip at the 'left luggage'.
A smart policeman told me a house to try.

In dim-lit streets, war-tired people moved slowly
like dark-coated bears in a snowy region.
I in my Caribbean gear
was a half-finished shack in the cold winds.
In November, the town was a frosty field.
I walked fantastic stone streets in a dream.

A man on duty took my ten-shilling note
for a bed for four nights.
Inflated with happiness I followed him.
I was left in a close-walled room,
left with a dying shadeless bulb,
a pillowless bed and a smelly army blanket –
all the comfort I had paid for.

Curtainless in morning light, I crawled out of bed
onto wooden legs and stiff-armed body,
with a frosty-board face that I patted
with icy water at the lavatory tap.

Then I came to fellow-inmates in a crowded room.
A rage of combined smells attacked me,
clogging my nostrils –
and new charges of other smells merely
increased the stench. I was alone.
I alone was nauseated and choked in deadly air.

One-legged people stood around a wall of hot plates
prodding sizzled bacon and kippers.
Sore-legged and bandaged people poured tea.
Weather-cracked faces, hairy and hairless, were chewing.
No woman smiled. No man chuckled.
Words pressed through gums and gaps of rusty teeth.

Grimy bundles and bags were pets
beside grimy bulges of people, bowed, and in little clusters.
Though ever so gullible I knew – this was a dosshouse.
I collected back seven shillings and sixpence.
I left the place and its smells, their taste still with me
and again instinct directed me.

I walked without map, without knowledge
from Victoria to Brixton. On Coldharbour Lane
I saw a queue of men – some black –
and stopped. I stood by one man in the queue.
'Wha happenin brodda? Wha happenin here?'

Looking at me he said 'You mus be a jus-come?
You did hear about Labour Exchange?' 'Yes – I hear.'
'Well, you at it! But, you need a place whey you live.'
He pointed. 'Go over dere and get a room.'
So, I had begun – begun in London.

Hymn to New Day Arriving

Now – watch this new day arriving,
this glorious world ship coming silently
on the old, old waterway,
bringing the opening of light to seemingly settle.

Oh watch the ancient eye widening
to stir echoes, movements, voices,
to wake up all dormant life,
to tell flowers and faces to open.

Know this day will arouse some peace,
will express vigour to grow,
but, oh, will unleash merciless debt callers,
will corrode the energy of love.

Oh think of sweet first loves that will rot
and those that will flame like bright leaves.
Think of the finished work, standing like a building,
and the empty work that drains out hope.

New day is a turned-over book page,
new day renews spirit of energy.
Just like a little fresh cool breeze
new day invigorates with new life.

Then remember this
is only another day arriving,
coming with its new arousals
and despatching lives of completed time.

Oh how everything has its movement, its voice, its ending –
it is overwhelming.

Poems for Children

Seeing Granny

Toothless, she kisses
with fleshy lips
rounded, like mouth
of a bottle, all wet.

She bruises your face
almost, with two
loving tree-root hands.

She makes you sit, fixed.
She then stuffs you
with boiled pudding and lemonade.

She watches you feed
on her food. She milks
you dry of answers
about the goat she gave you.

Listn Big Brodda Dread, Na!

My sista is younga than me.
My sista outsmart five-foot-three.
My sista is own car repairer
and yu nah catch me doin judo with her.

    I sey I wohn get a complex
    I wohn get a complex
    Then I see the muscles my sista flex.

My sista is tops at disco dance.
My sista is well into self-reliance.
My sista plays guitar and drums
and wahn see her knock back double rums.

I sey I wohn get a complex
I wohn get a complex
Then I see the muscles my sista flex.

My sista doesn mind smears of grease and dirt.
My sista'll reduce yu with sheer muscle hurt.
My sista says no guy goin keep her phone-bound –
with own car mi sista is a wheel-hound.

I sey I wohn get a complex
I wohn get a complex
Then I see the muscles my sista flex.

Scribbled Notes Picked Up by Owners, and Rewritten
because of bad grammar, bad spelling, bad writing

Letter signed – YOUR ONE BABY-PERSON.

I know you like me
because you know I like to be tossed up
in the air and caught
and I know you're best
at making laughs.
You know it's great
when you coo and coo on me in smiles
with hugs and tickles and teases.
I rub my legs together.
I do my baby-dance on my back.
My fist hangs on your thumb.
I chuckle. I chuckle, saying
'This face over me is great!'
I say GA, GA, and you know I say
Go-Ahead, Go-Ahead. Make
funny faces talk, sing,
tickle. Please. Make me chuckle
this time, next time,
every time. Now. Please.

Letter signed – YOUR SPECIAL-BIG-PUPPY-DOG.

You know I'm so big
I'll soon become a person.
You know I want to know more
of all that you know. Yet
you leave the house, so, so often.
And not one quarrel between us.
Why don't you come home ten times
a day? Come tell me the way
your boss is bad? See me sit,
listening, sad? And you know,
and I know, it's best
when you first come in.
You call my name. And O
I go starry-eyed on you,
can't stop wagging, jumping,
holding, licking your face,
saying, 'D'you know – d'you know –
you're quite, quite a dish!'
Come home – come call my name –
every time thirty minutes pass.

Letter from KITTEN-CAT-ALMOST-BIG-CAT.

You tell me to clear up
the strings of wool off
the floor, just to see how
I slink out the door. But O
you're my mum. Fifty times
big to climb on. You stroke
my back from head to tail.
You tickle my furry throat,
letting my claws needle your side,
and my teeth nibble your hand
till I go quiet. I purr.
I purr like a poor boy
snoring, after gift of a dinner.
I leap into your lap only
to start everything over.

From YOUR COLOURFUL-GUINEA-PIG.

You come to me. I shriek
to you, to let you know
I'm a found friend
you can depend on. I know
you long to learn my language.
You talk to me over
and over, in lots
of little words. I listen,
going still, with a quiet heart.
My eyes should go
all in a brighter shine.
Watch my eyes.
Listen to my shriek.
You'll hear what I say.

Letter from YOUR RABBIT.

To you, who belongs to me.
I listen. You know that.
Come see me. Now.
After. Soon. Later. Again.
All Time – talk
with same words you bring
on my face like daybreak
everyday. Stroke me like wind
passing. Then you've come
for heads to be lost together
in a hole in the ground,
in dreams about fields
grown and overgrown.
Watch my ears, you'll see
I catch all you say.
Feel my eyes on you
and you'll hear
'I have space for you
to huddle, in my bed.'

Letter from YOUR horse.

Though I'm sort of high up and big
I don't boast. I'm not snooty.
I don't get easily cross.
When you come to me, come
with a long rope of talk
like I'm a soppy dog.
Stroke me with looks, voice,
hands, together saying,
'Hello big fellow!
Handsome big fellow,
you're a joy on the eye
with broad back under sky.
You're swift like flits
of lightning lifts of feet,
but stand still
to listen to human parrot.'
You talk like that,
I nuzzle you,
Hear when I say,
'Come walk with me,
clop–clopping,
with me, side by side.'

You see, I sign a letter myself PIG.

But O most of all
I want you to see
I want us to dig together,
wallow together and share
one bath. I want us to talk
together, all muddy and smart.
I want you to have
my work and my fun.
You give me food, you're gone.
You'll forget and forget and forget
that if you scratch my back
or rub my belly on and on,
ever so weak I go.
I lie down. I stretch out.

I grunt. I grunt, saying
'Don't. Don't. Don't.
Don't you stop stroking.'

Black Kid in a New Place

I'm here, I see
I make a part of a little planet
here, with some of everybody now.

I stretch myself, I see
I'm like a migrant bird
who will not return from here.

I shake out colourful wings.
I set up a palmtree bluesky
here, where winter mists were.

Using what time tucked in me, I see
my body pops with dance.
Streets break out in carnival.

Rooms echo my voice. I see
I was not a migrant bird. I am
a transplanted sapling, here, blossoming.

A Story About Afiya

Afiya has fine black skin
that shows off her white clothes
and big brown eyes that laugh
and long limbs that play.
She has a white summer frock
she wears and washes every night
that every day picks on something
to collect, strangely.

Afiya passes sunflowers and finds
the yellow-fringed black faces there,
imprinted on her frock, all over.
Another time she passes red roses
and there the clustered bunches
are, imprinted on her frock.

She walks through high grass and sees
butterflies and all kinds
of slender stalks and petals
patterned on her back and front
and are still there, after
she has washed her dress.

Afiya stands. She watches
the sharp pictures in colour,
untouched by her wash.
Yet, next morning, every day,
the dress is cleaned and ready,
hanging white as new paper.

Then pigeons fly up before her
and decorate her dress
with their flight and group design.
Afiya goes to the zoo;
she comes back with two tigers
together, on her back and on her front.

She goes to the seaside;
she comes home with fishes
under ruffled waves
in the whole stretch of sea
imprinted on her dress.

She walks between round and towered
boulders and takes them away,
pictured on her.
Always Afiya is amazed,
just like when she comes home
and finds herself covered
with windswept leaves
of October, falling.

Afiya: a Swahili name, meaning health, is pronounced *Ah-fee-yah.*

When I Dance

When I dance it isn't merely
That music absorbs my shyness,
My laughter settles in my eyes,
My swings of arms convert my frills
As timing tunes my feet with floor
As if I never just looked on.

It is that when I dance
O music expands my hearing
And it wants no mathematics,
It wants no thinking, no speaking,
It only wants all my feeling
In with animation of place;

When I dance it isn't merely
That surprises dictate movements,
Other rhythms move my rhythms,
I uncradle rocking-memory
And skipping, hopping and running
All mix movements I balance in.

It is that when I dance
I'm costumed in a rainbow mood,
I'm okay at any angle,
Outfit of drums crowds madness round,
Talking winds and plucked strings conspire,
Beat after beat warms me like sun.

When I dance it isn't merely
I shift bodyweight balances
As movement amasses my show,
I celebrate each dancer here,
No sleep invades me now at all
And I see how I am tireless.

It is that when I dance
I gather up all my senses
Well into hearing and feeling,
With body's flexible postures
Telling their poetry in movement
And I celebrate all rhythms.

One

Only one of me
and nobody can get a second one
from a photocopy machine.

Nobody has the fingerprints I have.
Nobody can cry my tears, or laugh my laugh
or have my expectancy when I wait.

But anybody can mimic my dance with my dog.
Anybody can howl how I sing out of tune.
And mirrors can show me multiplied
many times, say, dressed up in red
or dressed up in grey.

Nobody can get into my clothes for me
or feel my fall for me, or do my running.
Nobody hears my music for me, either.

I am just this one.
Nobody else makes the words
I shape with sound, when I talk.

But anybody can act how I stutter in a rage.
Anybody can copy echoes I make.
And mirrors can show me multiplied
many times, say, dressed up in green
or dressed up in blue.

Boy Alone at Noon

Completely central over me
is this lace of sun
topping trees.

The world is white
and green and shadowy
I am almost enclosed from sky

180

The river lolls lapping
over rough tongued rocks
and leaf rottings

A dragonfly takes two dips
it flops in again
it goes with a flip

The nutmeg trees
have pods propped with nuts
I smell hot grass

I smell tree blossoms
I wish I could know
a lot of reasons

Busy birds go stateless
I have no government either
My father is strong and pocketless

The track waits to my hut
I better fill my bamboo with water
and go on up

Getting Nowhere

Next week I'll leave school.
Next week, nil, fulltime –
me – for good!

Yonks now
nobody bothered.
No teacher scrawled, 'work harder'.
Or, 'Use your potential'.

They'd twigged on.
Their words were whispers
to a rock. So
They gave up on me.

They had no grasp –
none to give.
Had no power to kick
my motor into clatter.

Not to lift a bat, next week
I'm bowled out for duck.
Year in year out
terrible need took
nothing teachers served.

I couldn't win them.
They couldn't win me.
Their mouthings reached me jammed.
So routines to me will end next week.

Lamp of workshop drawing got built
only as far as the base
and abandoned. Made scrap.

And a relief will grab them.
Relieved, the teachers will sigh –
'Clearly, a non-achiever.'

Next week, I'll leave school
but stay held on poverty street.
Held hostage by myself, they'll say.

It Seems I Test People

My skin sun-mixed like basic earth
my voice having tones of thunder
my laughter working all of me as I laugh
my walk motioning strong swings
it seems I test people

Always awaiting a move
waiting always to recreate my view
my eyes packed with hellos behind them
my arrival bringing departures
it seems I test people

What Do We Do with a Variation?

What do we do with a difference?
Do we stand and discuss its oddity
or do we ignore it?

Do we shut our eyes to it
or poke it with a stick?
Do we clobber it to death?

Do we move around it in rage
and enlist the rage of others?
Do we will it to go away?

Do we look at it in awe
or purely in wonderment?
Do we work for it to disappear?

Do we pass it stealthily
or change route away from it?
Do we will it to become like ourselves?

What do we do with a difference?
Do we communicate to it,
let application acknowledge it
for barriers to fall down?

Me Go a Granny Yard

Wha mek yu go Granny Yard?
       Me go Granny Yard
       fi go get sorrel drink.
An dat a really really true?
       Cahn yu hear a true?
Yu noh did go fi notn else?
       Dohn yu hear a notn else?

Wha mek yu go Granny Yard?
       Me go Granny Yard
       fi go get bwoil puddn.
An dat a really really true?
       Cahn yu hear a true?
Yu noh did go fi notn else?
       Dohn yu hear a notn else?

Wha mek yu go Granny Yard?
       Me go Granny Yard
       fi go get orange wine.
An dat a really really true?
       Cahn yu hear a true?
Yu noh did go fi notn else?
       Dohn yu hear a notn else?

Wha mek yu go Granny Yard?
       Me go Granny Yard
       fi go get cokenat cake.
An dat a really really true?
           Cahn yu hear a true?
Yu noh did go fi notn else?
       Dohn yu hear a notn else?

Wha mek yu go Granny Yard?
       Me go Granny Yard
       fi go get lemonade.
An dat a really really true?
           Cahn yu hear a true?
Yu noh did go fi notn else?
       Dohn yu hear a notn else?

Wha mek yu go Granny Yard?
    Me go Granny Yard
      fi go get ginger cookies.
An dat a really really true?
        Cahn yu hear a true?
Yu noh did go fi notn else?
      Dohn yu hear a notn else?

Wha mek yu go Granny Yard?
    Me go Granny Yard
      fi go hide from punishment.
Fi go hide from punishment?
      Fi go hide from punishment!

Jamaican Song

Little toad little toad mind yourself
mind yourself let me plant my corn
plant my corn to feed my horse
feed my horse to run my race –
the sea is full of more than I know
moon is bright like night time sun
night is dark like all eyes shut
    Mind – mind ya not harmed
    somody know bout yu
    somody know bout yu

Little toad little toad mind yourself
mind yourself let me build my house
build my house to be at home
be at home till I one day vanish –
the sea is full of more than I know
moon is bright like night time sun
night is dark like all eyes shut
    Mind – mind yu not harmed
    somody know bout yu
    somody know bout yu

Hurricane

Under low black clouds
the wind was all
speedy feet, all horns and breath,
all bangs, howls, rattles,
in every hen house,
church hall and school.

Roaring, screaming, returning,
it made forced entry, shoved walls,
made rifts, brought roofs down,
hitting rooms to sticks apart.

It wrung soft banana trees,
broke tough trunks of palms.
It pounded vines of yams,
left fields battered up.

Invisible with such ecstasy –
with no intervention of sun or man
everywhere kept changing branches.

Zinc sheets are kites.
Leaves are panic swarms.
Fowls are fixed with feathers turned.
Goats, dogs, pigs,
all are people together.

Then growling it slunk away
from muddy, mossy trail and boats
in hedges: arid cows, ratbats, trees,
fish, all dead in the road.

Isn't My Name Magical?

Nobody can see my name on me.
My name is inside
and all over me, unseen
like other people also keep it.
Isn't my name magical?

My name is mine only.
It tells I am individual,
the one special person it shakes
when I'm wanted.

Even if someone else answers
for me, my message hangs in air
haunting others, till it stops
with me, the right name.
Isn't your name and my name magic?

If I'm with hundreds of people
and my name gets called,
my sound switches me on to answer
like it was my human electricity.

My name echoes across playground
It comes, it demands my attention.
I have to find out who calls,
who wants me for what.
My name gets blurted out in class,
it is terror, at a bad time,
because somebody is cross.

My name gets called in a whisper
I am happy, because
My name may have touched me
with a loving voice.
Isn't your name and my name magic?

Childhood Tracks

Eating crisp fried fish with plain bread.
Eating sheared ice made into 'snowball'
with syrup in a glass.
Eating young jelly-coconut, mixed
with village-made wet sugar.
Drinking cool water from a calabash gourd
on worked land in the hills.

Smelling a patch of fermenting pineapples
in stillness of hot sunlight.
Smelling mixed whiffs of fish, mango, coffee,
mint, hanging in a market.
Smelling sweaty padding lifted off a donkey's back.

Hearing a nightingale in song
in moonlight and sea-sound.
Hearing dawn-crowing of cocks, in answer
to others around the village.
Hearing the laughter
of barefoot children carrying water.
Hearing a distant braying of a donkey
in a silent hot afternoon.
Hearing palmtrees' leaves rattle
on and on at Christmas time.

Seeing a woman walking in loose floral frock.
Seeing a village workman with bag and machete
under a tree, resting, sweat-washed.
Seeing a tangled land-piece of banana trees
with goats in shades cud-chewing
Seeing a coil of plaited tobacco
like rope, sold, going in bits.
Seeing children playing in schoolyard
between palm and almond trees.
Seeing children toy-making in a yard
while slants of evening sunlight slowly disappear.
Seeing an evening's dusky hour lit up
by dotted lamplight.
Seeing fishing nets repaired between canoes.

Rain Friend

All alone out-a deep darkness
two mile from Aunt Daphne
little Dearie – knee high little Dearie –
come push door open,
sodden with rain to hair root
all through to thin black skin
from naked foot bottom.

And she stand up there giggling.
A-say she did like the sea
the sky throw pon her,
coming down all over her
like say all her friends in it too
running about pasture and dark trees.

And when she did close her eyes and laugh
she hear Cousin Joe Jackass braying
and Great House dog them barking
and road-water carry and carry her
like she a sailing boat in darkness.

Okay, Brown Girl, Okay

for Josie, nine years old, who wrote to me saying,
'Boys called me names because of my colour. I felt very upset
...my brother and sister are English. I wish I was, then
I won't be picked on... How do you like being brown?'

Josie, Josie, I am okay
being brown. I remember,
every day dusk and dawn get born
from the loving of night and light
who work together, like married.
　　　And they would like to say to you:
　　　Be at school on and on, brown Josie
　　　like thousands and thousands and thousands
　　　of children, who are brown and white
　　　and black and pale-lemon colour.
　　　All the time, brown girl Josie is okay.

Josie, Josie, I am okay
being brown. I remember,
every minute sun in the sky
and ground of the earth work together
like married.
　　　And they would like to say to you:
　　　Ride on up a going escalator
　　　like thousands and thousands and thousands
　　　of people, who are brown and white
　　　and black and pale-lemon colour.
　　　All the time, brown girl Josie is okay.

Josie, Josie, I am okay
being brown. I remember,
all the time bright-sky and brown-earth
work together, like married
making forests and food and flowers and rain.
　　　And they would like to say to you:
　　　Grow and grow brightly, brown girl.
　　　Write and read and play and work.
　　　Ride bus or train or boat or aeroplane
　　　like thousands and thousands and thousands
　　　of children, who are brown and white
　　　and black and pale-lemon colour.
　　　All the time, brown girl Josie is okay.

Innercity Youth Walk and Talks

He walks along with me and talks.
Says, 'Yes. I'm a fulltime
graffiti artist, and busy
with a real job what I like.'

Says, 'My style's my own style.
All artists know my work
and could get my message
on wall, in train, in bus,
on chimney, lamppost,
drainpipe, pavement, wherever.'

He says, 'I baffle heads of the town
with strategic secret signs.
Gives me a real buzz that.
Indoors sitting down.
How my art strikes people
just for the look at it.

'Satisfaction work that.
Takes art to the public.
Makes you vegetarian.

'For a lift inside and a cool
my dad settled on "the weed".
For a lift inside and a cool
I look for fresh work ideas.
To hide from faces
my dad lives in dark glasses.
To hide from faces, I look up
my night-time secret work.

'Yes,' he says. 'Risk of the job is
the risk of any job.
A work with height and depth
keeps eyes open round the head
for rail repairmen coming
or light of train dashing up
and keeps you nippy as a rat.'

Says, 'My mom took to a wig
to look like Tina Turner.
Mister Big my brother swears
nobody likes him
and he's stuck with that.
My dad doesn't get a pay,
doesn't get praises,
respect or adventure.
I make art in danger places.
And it's a buzz travelling daytime
seeing my secret signs everywhere.'

Says, 'Everybody has a downside
My downside takes to height.
Nobody in my family took to art.
Why not go for it I said.'

Says, 'Managed big gold buckle belt
with head of African king on it.
But I want a Suzuki bike
and can't manage it.
So I go for getting grimed
in city rubbish in corners.
Getting stuck between walls.
But it's a satisfaction work.'

Trick a Duppy

If you wahn trick a duppy
and wahn walk on *happy happy*
in a moonshine – bright moonshine –
hear how and how things work out fine.

You see duppy. No whisper. No shout.
Make not the least sound from you mouth.
One after the other *straight straight*,
strike three matchsticks alight.
Drop one then two of the sticks ablaze
and before you walk a steady pace
flash dead last match like you drop it
when *smart smart* it slipped in you pocket
to have duppy haunted in a spell
and why so you cannot tell.

But duppy search search for third matchstick
to vanish only when 6 a.m. come tick.

duppy: a ghost.

Love Is Like Vessel

Love is like vessel
that is mother and is father
and is nature parts
that become pure water.

Love is like face of ground
kissing feet
under whatever
bodyweight it greets.

It is like elements
that together make night
and elements
that together make light.

193

It is like carrying
a head that makes no weight
and also like quiet warmth
around cold hate.

Love is like finished work
with mixes so well wed
that grain, milk, yeast, heat are balanced
offering a *fine fine* bread.

Love is like roundness
of a running wheel
over a bumpy road
or one simply smooth like steel.

People Equal

Some people shoot up tall.
Some hardly leave the ground at all.
        Yet – people equal. Equal.

One voice is a sweet mango.
Another is a non-sugar tomato.
        Yet – people equal. Equal.

Some people rush to the front.
Others hang back, feeling they can't.
        Yet – people equal. Equal.

Hammer some people, you meet a wall
        Blow hard on others they fall.
        Yet – people equal. Equal.

One person will aim at a star.
        For another, a hilltop is *too far*.
        Yet – people equal. Equal.

Some people get on with their show.
Others never get on the go.
        Yet – people equal. Equal.

Gobble-Gobble Rap

Me do a whispa and a big shout
with a meat-and-a-sweet mouth
like a non-meat, non-fish, puddn mouth
which is – a sleeper-waker, want-it-want-it mouth
which is – a take it, break it, eater mouth
which is – a gobble-gobble mouth

Me do a whispa and a big shout
with an oily-oily, salty-pepper mouth
like any seafood, wing-food, ground-food mouth
which is – a want-more-now, want-more-now mouth
which is – a chopper-chopper, swallow-down mouth
which is – a gobble-gobble mouth

Me do a whispa and a big shout
with a bony-and-a-fleshy meaty mouth
like a buttered-up, creamed up, oiled-up mouth
which is – a smile-and-smile, fries-and-fish mouth
which is a loud, bossy-bossy mouth
which is – a gobble-gobble mouth

Me do a whispa and a big shout
with a bun-and-cake and ice cream mouth
like a shopping for a cupboard mouth
which is – a mouthy, eat-eat, noisy mouth
which is – a break-it-up, bite-it-up mouth
which is – a gobble-gobble mouth.

Me do a whispa and a big shout
with a pie, chocolate and apple mouth
like any chatty-chatty, suck-sweet mouth
which is – a on-and-off, laugh-and-laugh mouth
which is – a gimme-gimme-more mouth
which is – a gobble-gobble mouth.

Me do a whispa and a big shout
with always that ready mouth about
like even that slurper-burper mouth
which is – a raver-craver, seeker mouth
which is – a singer and kissy-kissy mouth
which is – a gobble-gobble mouth
    which is – a gobble-gobble mouth.

A Nest Full of Stars

Only chance made me come and find
my hen, stepping from her hidden
nest, in our kitchen garden.

In her clever secret place, her tenth
egg, still warm, had just been dropped.

Not sure of what to do, I picked up
every egg, counting them; then put them
down again. *All were mine.*

All swept me away and back.
I blinked, I saw: a whole hand
of ripe bananas, nesting.

I blinked, I saw: a basketful
of ripe oranges, nesting.

I blinked, I saw: a trayful
of ripe naseberries, nesting.

I blinked, I saw: an open bagful
of ripe mangoes, nesting.

I blinked, I saw:
a mighty nest full of stars.

Caribbean Playground Song

Say, Good mornin, Granny Maama
Good mornin, Granpa Taata.
    Good mornin when it rainin.
    Good mornin when sun shinin.
        Good mornin.

Say, Good mornin, Miss Pretty-Pretty.
Good mornin, one-yeye Mista Shorty.
    Good mornin when sun shinin.
    Good mornin when hurrikaanin
        Good mornin.

Say, Good mornin, Mista Big-N-Fat-Man.
Good mornin, Mista Maaga Man.
    Good mornin when sun shinin.
    Good mornin when hurrikaanin
        Good mornin.

Say, Good mornin, Mista Lamefoot
Good mornin, dear Miss No-Toot.
Good mornin when sun shinin.
    Good mornin when hurrikaanin
        Good mornin.

Say, Good mornin, dear-dear Bush Miss.
Good mornin, dear Mista Touris.
    Good mornin when sun shinin.
    Good mornin when hurrikaanin
        Good mornin.

Say, Good mornin, Granny Maama
Good mornin, Granpa Taata.
    Good mornin.

one-yeye: one-eyed; *Maaga:* meagre or thin; *No-Toot:* No-tooth; *Touris:* tourist.

Flop, Clonk, Bump, Zoom

Floppily, floppier, floppity, flop, flop.
Flippily, flippier, flippity, flip, flip.

Clonkily, clonkier, clonkity, clonk, clonk.
Clinkily, clinkier, clinkity, clink, clink.

Sloshily, sloshier, sloshity, slosh, slosh.
Splashily, splashier, splashity, splash, splash.

Bumpily, bumpier, bumpity, bump, bump.
Boomily, boomier, boomity, boom, boom.
Zoomily, zoomier, zoomity, zoom, zoom.

Tall Wide and Heavy

He was so big and so strong
as he walked along, sometimes
dry ground under him squelched
a fountain of water.
And squelched ground made him belch.

He was so wide and so tall
he was like a walking wall
sweeping things along
with his walk.
And as dogs bit him, their teeth broke.

Uncollected Poems

A Redefining

A black man says he has
no more smiles. He spent
all his grinning.

Each splendid piece of work
he does, makes him
a clown that climbed Everest,

Every perfect act he performs
gets adjudged a classic
sung by a dog.

Childhood Memory

Naked night sits around
the hut thin and dim
my mother strokes my head
and sings
to sweet smell of labour
from fields
and we pack round the floor
like gathered logs
and saplings thrown down
hour after hour
for the next full time of work
to keep the fruits
as the hot earth would
and the palms of every man
open as leaves
pockets bare as the trunks
branches curtaining the faces
every step as if
the strongest yearning we have
is to live like trees.

A Father's Vigil

He stayed home that night
with the deadly
black spider bite
in his big hand
his voice a groaning bass
patrolling the hut
to seize everybody
in the vice of his
shameless agony
with five sons awake
on the floor
in dim lamplight
aware of the tortured
shadow in calico shorts:
all wondering if they'd
miss him if he was
bones in the ground,
all knowing the beast,
he was to their mother,
and knowing his low
neighing of a chuckle
with cap against his chest
at the sight of a white face –
beneath himself completely,
seeing that hand
that held a lump of sugar.

Fatherhood

His response came in the special care
he gave to his pieces of green lands
with a few coconut, pimento and cedar trees
where his days passed in a mother love for a patch
of over-tended yam hills, a few spreading roots of sugarcane,
no more than a dozen roots of plantain trees,
a cricket-pitch length of pineapple patch.

He washed small children in his high pitch of a gentle voice,
giving sticky sweets and overripe fruits from his pockets.

He over-cared for a couple of cows,
over-oiled, combed and brushed a horse

and pampered himself, with his breaks in town
going fishing and rum drinking
and doing jobs for the old white woman estate owner for nothing.

No hunger for money ever getting into his blood
he frustrated us, his caring effusive but going like wind,
not making growing wealth.

His seeds grew, but not he who planted them.
His land was not prepared,
with his going on like he had no skills
to amass the light of his soul,
like a slave who could only
allow his light to be reaped and taken
as if he had no children.
So crisis lingered there, in my father,
a disquiet we could not lose.

Cos somtin mek it so

Bwoy mi tell yu
dis pipe yah
wha mi pull fram mout
mi cling to like love
yet mi know it a deputy fi somtn
de Laard alone know what.

Man-love tricky-tricky
cos man-love is sometimey.
Man-love is like sweetwood fire:
it blaze up quick-quick an done.

Woman-love pull man fi come
den woman-love turn
sharp tongue an kick-up an bust-up
cos woman have a love
to patch up everytin.

Bwoy mi tell yu
every tree have a job fi show
wha it can do wid sunshine
cos somtin mek it so.

An woman a-keep
blowin up fire
cos somtin mek it so, bwoy,
cos somtin mek it so.

Ol Nasty-Mout

When I a bwoy I did know
a big froggy eyed longleg
man in we distric. Dat
man woz a nasty-mout man.

An him didn jus av rude
talk. Him mout did draw
blue fly dem an a-throw
centipede and scorpion dem
wid de blue-light
him bad word dem pop.

Him mout did dirty bad bad!
An him bes time woz
to lectrocute an half kill mi
wid rude talk bout woman sweetnis.
An him coax me,
coax mi to listn more,
keeping him eye dem shinin
watchin me all halfdead.

Village Sex Lesson Number One

Bwoy, evva si woman born-part –
place yu come fram? Evva si it,
bwoy? Eh? Woman evva show yu? Eh?
Well, yu mus aaks. Speedy speedy
yu mus learn ow to aaks nice.
Yu av a special special voice to do
dat. No lady goin show yu she born-part
till yu use yu special special
voice. Hear mi, bwoy?
Hear wha big man a-tell yu?

An a wi warn yu. Like eyeball
every born-part look same, excep
fi colour, fi de love of life
an present expectation. But
kind-a mout lip dem wi tell yu
de size of de born-part. Always
de kind-a mout point dat out,
excep fi Chinese born-part, what is
crossway, like de mout. Rememba,
bwoy, wen yu pickin one,
de kind-a mout wi intraduce yu
to sweetis place on eart.

Hear wha I sey bwoy? An wen
woman show she born-part, rememba
yu not to frightn. I did know
a man who did frightn, an did
run straight home to question
him modda. I wi tell yu, bwoy,
de chop-up, chop-up look
of born-part is
de flower petal look of roses.

So young bwoy, yu hear ow
big man a-talk to yu, an a-tell yu
dat wen yu lickle young stick
get stiff pon yu a marnin time
is practice, it a practise
to please. An womankind av
a born-part to reach
sweet-water fram you neckback
to break it, an burn yu sweet sweet,
like heaven hol yu. Bwoy
evva break sweet water yet? Well
woman born-part a-go mek it happen.
Get big quick, bwoy. Get big quick.

Whatever happened to Miranda?

At seventeen
her tauntings marked me for life
the strength of her arms and wet wet kiss
her thighs that she showed in laughter like bells ringing
as she caught me and threw me away in high grass
and stood over me with skirts held high
and then ran and ran away
and never never could I catch her.

Man that girl marked me for life.
She aroused me, teased me,
but her big arms were there to guard her centre
and how marvellous Miranda would be
when altogether stirred up, I never knew.

And every time I went home I'd ask,
Whatever happened to Miranda?

God to Me

God to me man is
hot blood and juice in saps
crow of a cock strong as sun rays
seeds unwrapping trees

God to me man is
live sea-wave an return of sun
my own son turning man like me
his mumma company with me through life

God to me man is
life back of life
an eyes what see roun there
black and white skin an voice
darkness an stars

Absorbing

crossing mangrove swamps
and high branches tangled
like strong nests
with golden shower trees
and flameoftheforest in bloom
and creepers with variegated blobs
in white light hanging
and scattered like uneven coins
drowned in all sorts
of birds' voices
cracking twigs and layered leaves
I startled flocks
of ground doves
and bigger and smaller wings
time after time
till I came to clean wide sky
and like a lost cat climbed
a rockbound place
where the spine rushed
the river down the drop
of white waterfall
and not knowing whether
to listen to steady sunlight
the going on of uttering water
or tree parrots chattering
with an airy branch fanning my face
on a shelf of stone
comfortably prostrate
I fell asleep
alone in the world

Rough Sketch Beginning

I came to sketch
      my ideas for my picture

I saw the sun
      a bearded saint in bliss
      curled in a face of fire

I saw a mountain
      all a thought
      left standing there

I saw the sea
      a place too dreadful
      to be empty

I saw a river
      a lover fitted in
      a perfect slit

I saw woodland branches
      the many hands
      washing the wind

I saw birdsong
      colour streaks
      and circle pieces of the air

I saw dust
      dirt from our minds'
      uncleaned mirrors

I saw lightning
      chink of light from
      another world

I saw a storm
      peace unemployed
      turned into mischief

I saw night
      softest of world bedcover
      arousing passion